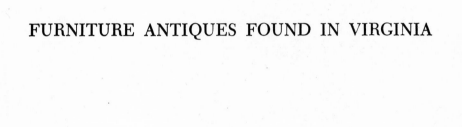

FURNITURE ANTIQUES FOUND IN VIRGINIA

(Photo by Lawrence D. Thornton)

Col. Fielding Lewis' study at Kenmore, Fredericksburg, Virginia

FURNITURE ANTIQUES FOUND IN VIRGINIA

A Book of Measured Drawings

By

ERNEST CARLYLE LYNCH, JR.

BONANZA BOOKS · NEW YORK

Library of Congress Catalog Card Number: 54–7784

Copyright, MCMLIV, The Bruce Publishing Company
Printed in the United States of America

This edition published by Bonanza Books,
a division of Crown Publishers, Inc., by
arrangement with the copyright owner
(A)

Dedicated to
my mother
LINDA HOLMES BEVERIDGE LYNCH
and to
HARRINGTON WADDELL
renowned Virginia educator

Carter's Grove, near Williamsburg, Virginia. One expects to find the grand mansion filled with antiques. Furniture treasures, however, are found in Virginia homes of all types: the grand house, the average home, farm homes, town houses, modern urban homes, and mountain cabins.

FOREWORD

For almost as many years as he can remember, the author has been fascinated by handsome old furniture with its graceful lines. He has been interested to see these ageless old pieces become as popular today as they were two hundred years ago. The details used by the old cabinetmakers therefore have been a source of study, and construction of reproductions in his own shop has been a natural consequence.

Growing out of this interest and study has been the realization that comparatively few of the old pieces have been put down on paper where they may serve as models or sources of inspiration. Furniture manufacturers have their designers who study old models and use them as source material for new creations. Museums are repositories for many fine examples of the work of early craftsmen, but little of this material is available to the school shop or to thousands of home-workshop craftsmen. Much of the material available emphasizes museum pieces to the exclusion of privately owned ones that, while sometimes not as perfect examples of a particular period, may be more suited to the needs of a family than those in a museum.

The purpose of this work, then, is to bring to readers a group of pieces not copied before, to give to craftsmen over the country a taste of the old furniture to be found in Virginia. Not all of the pieces were made in Virginia. It is often hard to say where an antique was made, but the antiques used in this collection were copied in the state of Virginia and are representative of the furniture in a great many Virginia homes. The original idea would have selected furniture from a group of Southern states, but so rich a vein of antiques awaits the prospector in the Old Dominion that pieces in other states must be the subject of future volumes.

The author wishes to thank those whose kindly help and friendly co-operation have made this a pleasant undertaking: Mildred N. Lynch, fellow craftsman and wife of the author, for help and advice in every phase of the work; Dr. Adolph G. Dittmar, Plattsburg, New York, for invaluable help with the photography; Mr. William Ball, Sr., West Chester, Pennsylvania, for permission to photograph reproduction brasses made by him; Dr. Leslie L. Campbell, Dr. and Mrs. J. J. Murray, Miss Penelope Graves, Dr. and Mrs. M. H. Stowe, Dr. Ruth L. Phillips, Mrs. J. L. Wright, Miss Stella Argenbright, Mr. and Mrs. R. Loring Cover, Mr. and Mrs. George Taylor, Mrs. C. L. Goodloe, Mr. and Mrs. D. L. Ashton, Mrs. W. W. Sproul, Miss Emma Byrd, Mrs. Thomas Deford, Mr. and Mrs. Charles Baker, Miss Miriam Bowman, and the Association for the Preservation of Virginia Antiquities for permission to copy some of the pieces appearing in these pages.

Grateful acknowledgment is made to Mrs. H. H. Smith, The Kenmore Association, and Mr. Lawrence D. Thornton for permission to use their photograph of a room at Kenmore, and to Mr. Philip Flournoy and the Virginia State Chamber of Commerce for permission to use a photograph of Carter's Grove.

Some of the furniture shown in this book came from cabins like this one.

INTRODUCTION

The furniture making up this collection has been measured, sketched, and photographed where found. Wherever possible, attention has been paid to inside or hidden details of construction, in order to convey to readers the joints and other ways of doing things used by early craftsmen.

Sometimes the author saw pieces completely disassembled in the shops of cabinetmakers overhauling or refinishing them. He was allowed to examine most of the furniture minutely, to determine the size of tenons and dovetails, the thickness of drawer sides, and a multitude of other details that throw light on the workmanship of olden times. In some instances detailed studies could not be made, and the author had to be content with only the visible lines and dimensions. In these cases he has used the same construction details that were in almost universal use long ago.

Dimensions have been given as found on the pieces and may be used to produce exact copies. The individual craftsman is free to change any or all of the dimensions of a piece. Some dimensions are impractical; some are clumsy or unnecessarily wasteful. Not many present-day craftsmen will want to put ¾-in. thick stock into the sides of a small table drawer or use ⅞-in. backing on a chest. Such changes will mean a few changes in the bills of materials. Other details may be changed; inlay may be left off, etc. The author could not make such changes and present the pieces as they are.

It is a thrilling fact that every piece of furniture portrayed in this book was made by hand with hand tools. Even the lathe was oftentimes turned by an apprentice at the great wheel. There were no power machines to speed the work of the artisan of a century and a half ago. Some communities had water-power up-and-down saws for sawing planks from logs, and sometimes a lathe was turned by water power; but the furniture of that day was handmade. There is not a sign of a machine having been used to produce any of this furniture. Knowing this, the accuracy with which old furniture was made is amazing, such as its squareness, the uniform thickness of chest tops and drawer fronts, and the exquisite marquetry and veneering. With all of our wonderful tools, we fail, often, to produce as excellent work.

The modern craftsman may want to emulate those old workmen and use only hand tools to fashion some of the pieces described here. He may be one of many who have few or no power tools at their command. It need not deter him. Here is a challenge. Here are opportunities to prove his skill as a handcraftsman. The man with a few good hand tools, a workbench and vise, a few clamps and a lathe (bought or homemade, powered by foot or motor), can reproduce every piece in this book.

We would not, of course, think of discarding power tools. They are grand things to have. Nevertheless, there does come to the worker with hand tools a wonderful sense of confidence in his skill and a satisfaction of accomplishment unmatched any other way. It is fine to have a mortising machine on which a perfect mortise can be made in an instant, but more self-confidence will be gained by making just as perfect a mortise with a chisel and mallet. So don't let the lack of a lot of power tools be a hindrance in having an immense amount of pleasurable work cutting and shaping wood into beautiful pieces of furniture.

Construction notes accompany the drawings. For detailed descriptions on the necessary steps in making various joints, besides other valuable information on many phases of woodshop work, consult woodworking books. Mr. Herman Hjorth's *Principles of Woodworking* contains explicit directions for making dovetail and other joints, using hand tools.

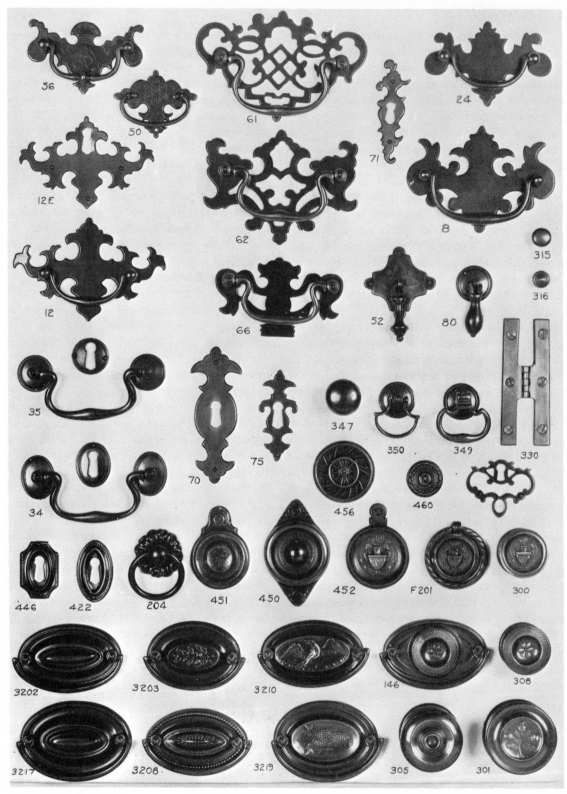

(Courtesy Wm. Ball, Sr., Ball Brasses)

Faithfully made reproduction brasses like these enhance the beauty of a carefully built piece of period furniture

10

CONTENTS

FURNITURE ANTIQUES FOUND IN VIRGINIA

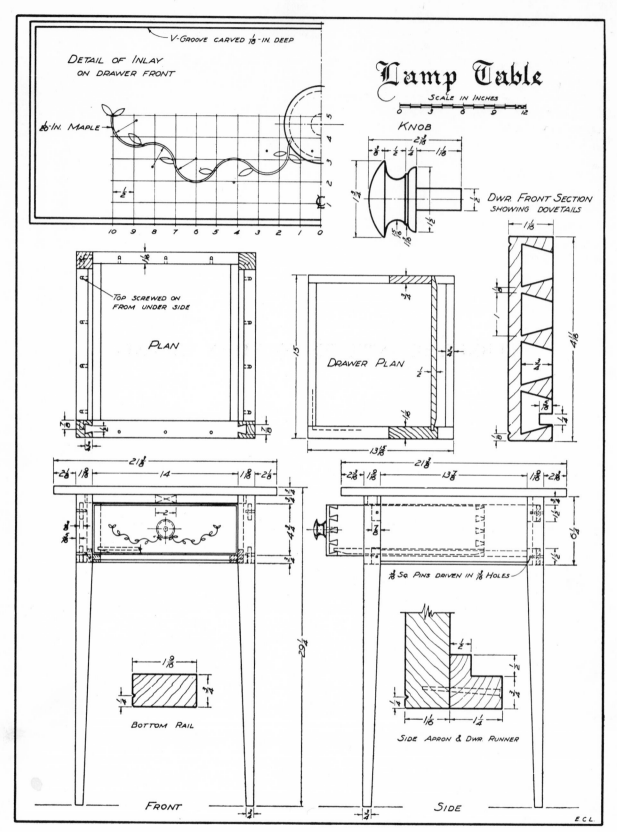

Lamp Table

SCALE IN INCHES

Detail of Inlay on Drawer Front

V-Groove carved ⅛-in. deep

⅛-In. Maple

Knob

Dwr. Front Section showing dovetails

Plan

Top screwed on from under side

Drawer Plan

Bottom Rail

Side Apron & Dwr. Runner

⅜ Sq. Pins driven in ⁵⁄₁₆ Holes

Front

Side

E.C.L.

PLATE 1

LAMP TABLE

Had the old cabinetmaker who made this little walnut table pasted a label under its top, reading "Made in Virginia," he could not have marked its origin much clearer than he did. Delicate vine inlay like this points to the Valley of Virginia and to the German and Swiss settlers in the upper part of that valley.

This table was copied in a farm home in Rockingham County. The couple who own it bought it twenty-odd years ago from a very old woman whose grandmother had owned it. Both parties to the transaction were pinched by the depression. The old woman was too proud to ask for a dole but put a price of fifty cents on the table (at the time painted blue). The farm wife who bought, being in a more fortunate position, gathered up an old hen, sold it for the required fifty cents, and completed the bargain. She confided to the author that she bought it just "to help out the old woman" and didn't discover her prize until years later when she decided to scrape off the old paint to repaint it.

CONSTRUCTION NOTES

1. Aside from the top, legs, and drawer runners, the various members are unnecessarily heavy and can be made thinner.

2. The V groove would indicate a true bead that had been flattened by scraping to refinish, but it actually appears never to have been a full rounded bead. However, a round bead molding will make a more finished job.

3. Although the inlay appears to be maple, do not hesitate to use 1/20 by 1/16-in. holly. Note that it was put in the narrow way. This is a fine job for a small high-speed router used with a pattern to guide its path.

4. After the knob was driven into the glue-coated hole in the drawer front, the 1/2-in. diameter tenon was split vertically and a thin wedge was driven in.

Bill of Materials

PIECES	ARTICLE	KIND OF WOOD	THICKNESS	WIDTH	LENGTH	REMARKS
1	Top	Walnut	3/4	21 3/8	21 3/8	
4	Legs	Walnut	1 9/16	1 9/16	28 1/2	Taper inside edges to 3/4 in.
2	Drawer rails	Walnut	3/4	1 9/16	15 1/2	14 in. between tenons
2	Side aprons	Walnut	1 1/16	6 1/4	15 5/8	13 7/8 in. between tenons
1	Back apron	Walnut	1 1/16	6 1/4	15 3/4	14 in. between tenons
2	Drawer runners	Pine	1 1/4	1 1/4	14 3/8	Shape as shown
1	Drawer top runner	Pine	3/4	2	14	Not on original
	Drawer					
1	Front	Walnut	1 1/16	4 11/16	13 15/16	Bead and inlay
2	Sides	Pine	3/4	4 11/16	14 11/16	
1	Back	Pine	3/4	4 1/16	13 15/16	
1	Bottom	Pine	1/2	14 1/4	12 15/16	
1	Knob	Walnut	1 3/4	1 3/4	3	Turn.

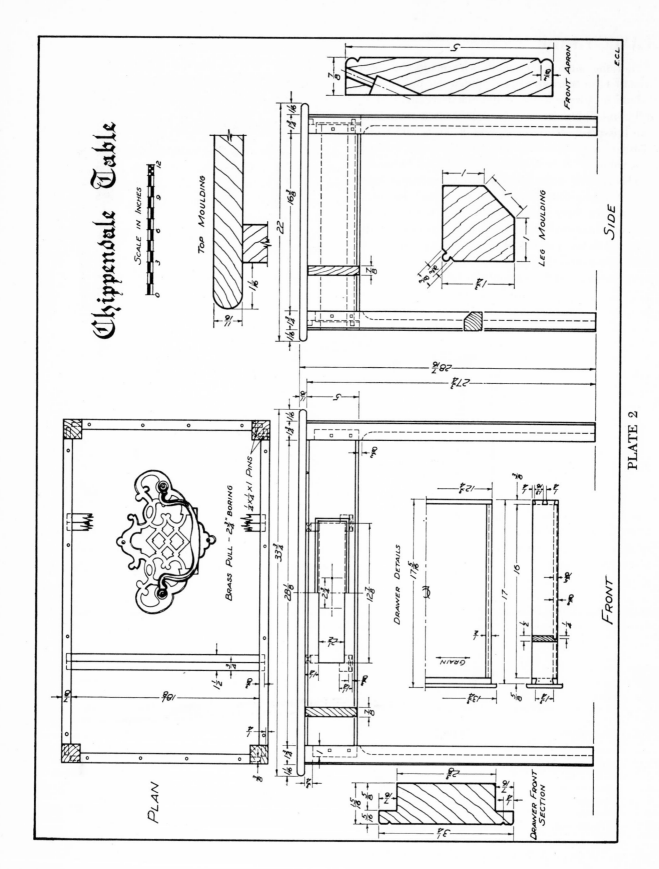

Chippendale Table

PLATE 2

CHIPPENDALE TABLE

This little table was originally at Kenmore, one of the handsomest estates in Virginia, but it, like the estate, had fallen into a sad state of disrepair before kindly and appreciative hands restored it to much of its former magnificence.

When the author first saw the table, its owner having brought it to a cabinet shop to be restored, it was a pitiable sight and ready and willing to fall into a dozen pieces. The pins had rotted, leaving the legs as wobbly as a newborn calf; the top was warped and cupped; the drawer pull was gone; and what little finish was left was old green paint.

Paint remover brought to view the design of the drawer pull as closely resembling the one shown in the drawing.[1] The weathered walnut around the pull was much lighter than the rich brown outlining the pull.

CONSTRUCTION NOTES

1. The drawer bottom nails up into rabbets on each side. It will make a better job to rabbet it, also, into the front. Better still, disregard the whole idea some old slave had about drawer building and use grooved joints.

2. A scratch stock will do all beading; a chisel will stop the leg chamfers.

---

[1] Wm. Ball, Sr., No. 61 Drawer Pull.

Bill of Materials

PIECES	ARTICLE	KIND OF WOOD	THICKNESS	WIDTH	LENGTH	REMARKS
1	Top	Walnut	$1\frac{1}{16}$	22	$33\frac{3}{4}$	
4	Legs	Walnut	$1\frac{3}{4}$	$1\frac{3}{4}$	$27\frac{3}{4}$	
2	Aprons, front and back	Walnut	$\frac{7}{8}$	5	$30\frac{1}{8}$	$28\frac{1}{8}$ in. between tenons. Cut out one for drawer.
2	Side aprons	Walnut	$\frac{7}{8}$	5	$18\frac{3}{8}$	$16\frac{3}{8}$ in. between tenons
	Drawer					
1	Front	Walnut	$1\frac{5}{16}$	$3\frac{1}{4}$	$13\frac{3}{4}$	
2	Sides	Pine	$\frac{1}{2}$	$2\frac{3}{8}$	17	
1	Back	Pine	$\frac{3}{8}$	$2\frac{3}{8}$	$12\frac{3}{4}$	
1	Bottom	Pine	$\frac{5}{16}$	16	$12\frac{1}{4}$	
2	Runners	Pine	$1\frac{1}{4}$	$1\frac{1}{2}$	$18\frac{7}{8}$	$18\frac{1}{8}$ in. between tenons
2	Top runners	Pine	$\frac{3}{4}$	$1\frac{1}{4}$	$18\frac{7}{8}$	$18\frac{1}{8}$ in. between tenons
16	Pins	Walnut	$\frac{1}{4}$	$\frac{1}{4}$	$1\frac{1}{2}$	

Hardware: 1 drawer pull, $2\frac{3}{4}$-in. bore (Wm. Ball, No. 61)

17

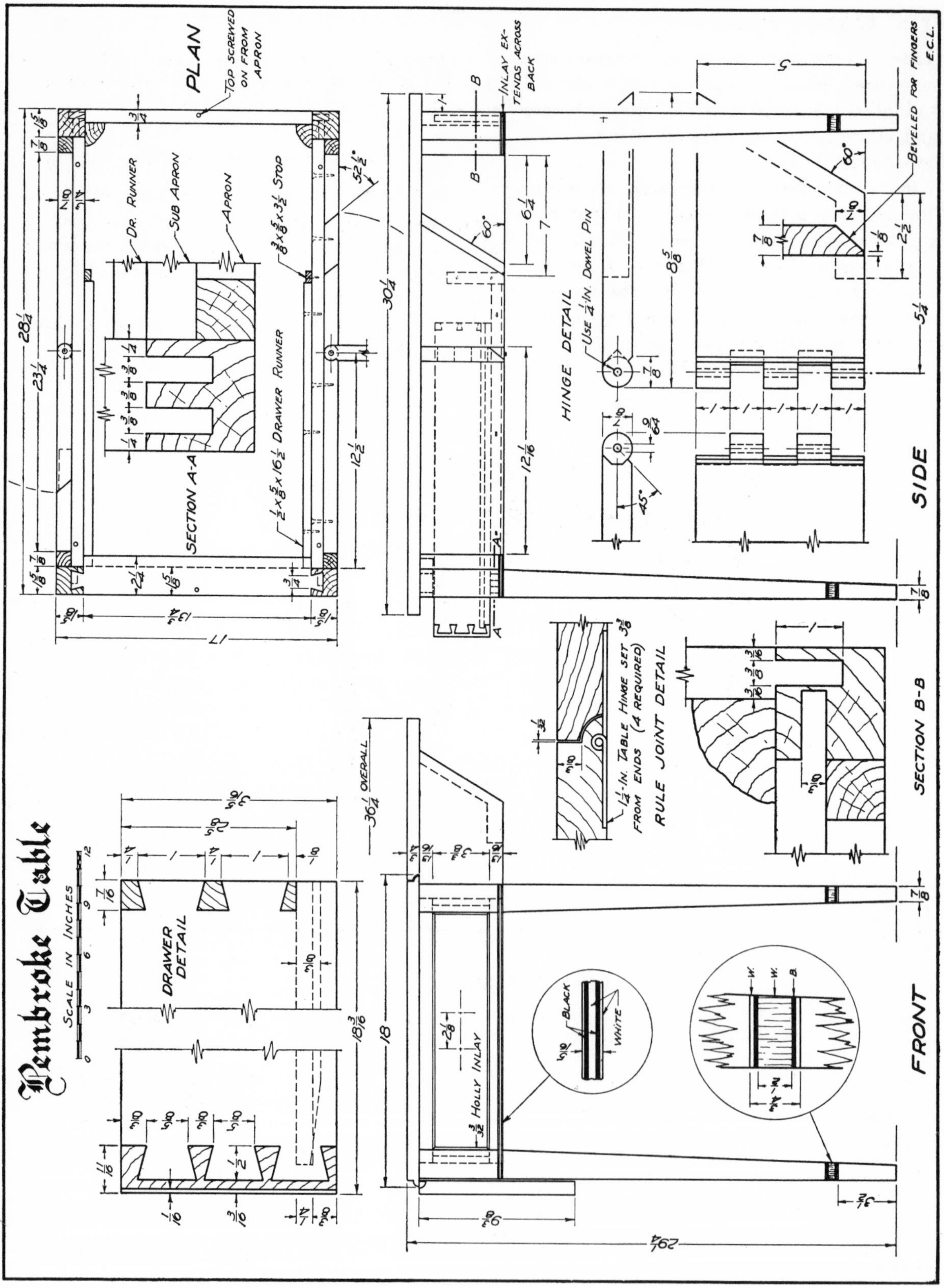
Pembroke Table
SCALE IN INCHES
DRAWER DETAIL
PLAN
TOP SCREWED ON FROM APRON
DR. RUNNER
SUB APRON
APRON
SECTION A-A
1/2 x 5/8 x 16 1/2 DRAWER RUNNER
3/8 x 5/8 x 3 1/2 STOP
INLAY EXTENDS ACROSS BACK
HINGE DETAIL
USE 1/4-IN. DOWEL PIN
SIDE
BEVELED FOR FINGERS
E.C.L.
36 1/4 OVERALL
1 1/4-IN. TABLE HINGE SET 3 3/8 FROM ENDS (4 REQUIRED)
RULE JOINT DETAIL
SECTION B-B
HOLLY INLAY
BLACK
WHITE
FRONT

PLATE 3

PEMBROKE TABLE

During the time of Hepplewhite, slender grace-fulness in design was the rule. His influence was tremendous; almost every article of furniture felt it, the numerous small tables called Pembroke not excepted. Said to be so named because the Countess of Pembroke had one made to her order, their number and the variety of their line and decoration are amazing. They are drop-leaf tables, smaller and daintier than those used for dining purposes, and their leaves are supported by the leaf of a wooden hinge, rather than by additional legs.

Made to serve a number of uses, most of them ornamental in part, they have ever been the delight of the builder who has a flair for inlay, crotch veneer, and oval, serpentine, or other shaped tops. Never expecting to find two exactly alike, they will be seen in great variety, some exquisite and complicated.

This table is of black walnut with walnut burl veneer on the drawer front.

CONSTRUCTION NOTES

1. When the table hinges are set flush with the surface and the leaves are down, as with this table, the gains show and break the line of the rule joint. If the hinges are fastened to the undersurface of the top and leaves, and the knuckle alone is gained into the top, the appearance, leaves down, will be improved.

2. Note the pieces, $\frac{7}{8}$ by $\frac{7}{8}$ by 5 in., glued onto the apron between the leg and the outer apron or hinge. Unless one's idea is to build a replica, these filler strips may be omitted and the fixed hinge pieces lengthened accordingly.

Bill of Materials

PIECES	ARTICLE	KIND OF WOOD	THICKNESS	WIDTH	LENGTH	REMARKS
1	Fixed top	Walnut	$\frac{3}{4}$	18	$30\frac{1}{4}$	
2	Leaves	Walnut	$\frac{3}{4}$	$9\frac{3}{8}$	$30\frac{1}{4}$	
4	Legs	Walnut	$1\frac{5}{8}$	$1\frac{5}{8}$	$28\frac{1}{2}$	
1	Back apron	Walnut	$\frac{3}{4}$	5	$15\frac{3}{4}$	$13\frac{3}{4}$ in. between tenons
1	Drawer rail	Walnut	$\frac{13}{16}$	$2\frac{1}{4}$	$15\frac{1}{4}$	$13\frac{3}{4}$ in. between dovetails
1	Drawer rail	Walnut	$\frac{13}{16}$	$1\frac{5}{8}$	$15\frac{3}{4}$	$13\frac{3}{4}$ in. between tenons
2	Aprons	Yellow pine	$\frac{3}{4}$	5	27	25 in. between tenons
2	Fixed hinge leaves	Walnut	$\frac{7}{8}$	5	$12\frac{1}{16}$	
2	Swing hinged leaves	Walnut	$\frac{7}{8}$	5	$8\frac{7}{8}$	
2	Filler pieces	Walnut	$\frac{7}{8}$	5	7	Bevel as shown.
4	Filler strips	Walnut	$\frac{7}{8}$	$\frac{7}{8}$	5	
2	Drawer runners	Yellow pine	$\frac{1}{2}$	$\frac{5}{8}$	$16\frac{1}{2}$	
2	Drawer top runners	Yellow pine	$\frac{1}{2}$	$\frac{13}{16}$	$16\frac{1}{2}$	Not on original but a useful addition.
2	Drawer stops	Yellow pine	$\frac{3}{8}$	$\frac{5}{8}$	$3\frac{1}{2}$	
	Drawer					
1	Front	Walnut	$1\frac{1}{16}$	$3\frac{5}{16}$	$13\frac{11}{16}$	
2	Sides	Yellow pine	$\frac{7}{16}$	$3\frac{5}{16}$	18	
1	Back	Yellow pine	$\frac{7}{16}$	$2\frac{5}{8}$	$13\frac{11}{16}$	
1	Bottom	Yellow pine	$\frac{3}{8}$	$13\frac{5}{16}$	$17\frac{3}{4}$	

Hardware: 1 drawer pull (Ball, No. 3208, $2\frac{3}{8}$-in. bore); 2 pcs. $\frac{1}{4}$ by 5 wood dowel for wooden hinge pins; 4 table hinges, $1\frac{1}{4}$ in. long

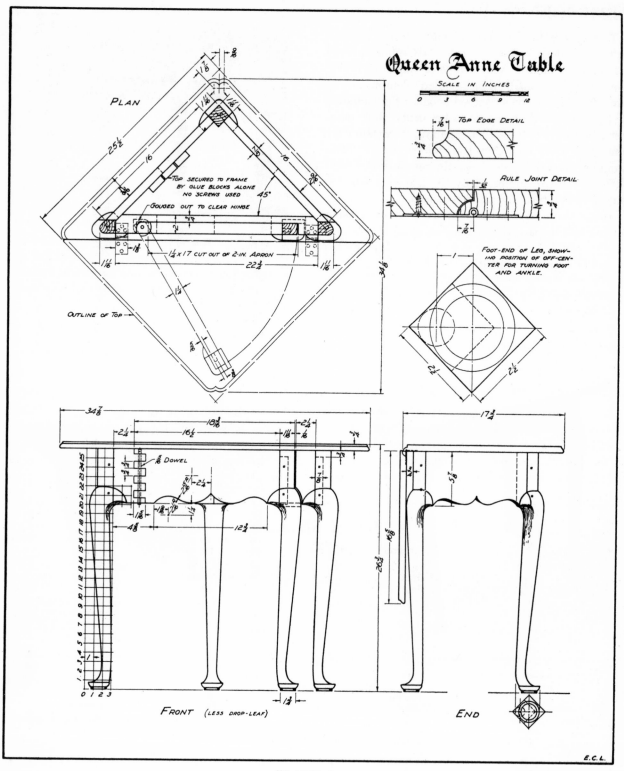

PLATE 4

QUEEN ANNE TABLE

The triangular shape of this card table gave it the name "corner table." It was also spoken of as "handkerchief table." It was a popular table found in many states around the middle of the eighteenth century, but it is quite rare now. Mahogany as well as walnut was used.

It is an interesting piece and will appeal to readers as "just the piece for that corner," but its practical use as a card table in this age of long-legged men and women is limited. The aprons are too low, allowing scant knee room.

CONSTRUCTION NOTES

1. Lumber can be saved by cutting top and leaf boards on an angle of 45 deg., but edge joints should be made carefully if only one clamp is to be used for each section.

2. Few builders will have 2-in. walnut to waste on the apron of a table and will substitute ⅞-in. walnut for the hinge, and back it up with ¾- or ⅞-in. pine or oak. Remember, when this table was built, it was thought that our forests were inexhaustible and gorgeous walnuts and cherries along with all other species were felled in windrows and burned to clear the land. No wonder the Indians fought the white man!

3. Legs have raised pad feet that may be turned on a lathe as described in the notes on the Queen Anne Side Chair, or they may be worked out by hand.

4. The frame is assembled before the knee blocks are fitted and glued in place. After the glue has set, they are filed and sanded smooth and flush. Patterns made to mark these blocks both ways will help make them uniform.

Bill of Materials

PIECES	ARTICLE	KIND OF WOOD	THICKNESS	WIDTH	LENGTH	REMARKS
1	Top	Walnut	¾	17¾	34⅞	After rule joint, top is approximately 25½ by 25½.
1	Leaf	Walnut	¾	16⅝	34⅜	
4	Legs	Walnut	2½	2½	26	
6	Leg blocks	Walnut	⅝	1⅝	2	
1	Leg block	Walnut	⅝	1¼	2	
2	Aprons	Walnut	⅞	5⅞	17¾	16 in. between tenons
1	Apron	Walnut	2	5⅞	24½	22¾ in. between tenons
1	Hinge	Walnut	1¼	5⅞	17⅜	⅞-in. tenon on one end

Hardware: 2 table hinges, 1¼ in. (Stanley, No. 819)

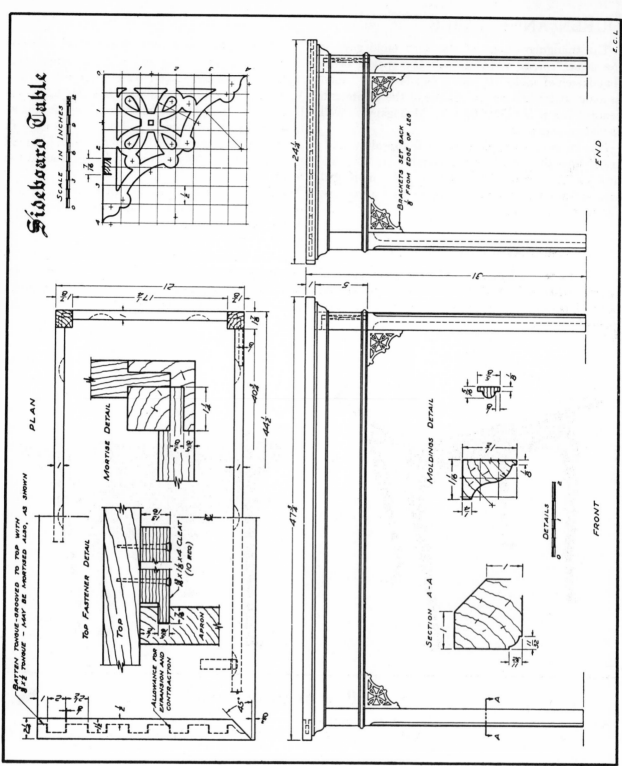

Sideboard Table

PLATE 5

SIDEBOARD TABLE

Similar to the one on Plate 35 in Thomas Chippendale's *Gentleman and Cabinet Maker's Director,* this table is shown in the book *Southern Antiques* by Paul H. Burroughs. It was a popular type in the South where it was variously known as a side, sideboard, or huntboard table. It is large enough to be used as a sideboard or, with appropriate architecture, as a dignified communion table for a church. Thought of as scaled down to a small size, many uses suggest themselves for a design of such charm.

CONSTRUCTION NOTES

The detail of a way to fasten the batten to the table-top ends is the author's suggestion. A 3/8 by 1/2-in. tongue on each end of the top engaging a groove in the battens was clearly visible. The rest is surmise based on similar cases where battens were removed, disclosing this method of construction. As a matter of fact, a fine job can be made leaving off the battens entirely but taking pains to sand carefully and double fill the exposed end grain.

Bill of Materials

PIECES	ARTICLE	KIND OF WOOD	THICKNESS	WIDTH	LENGTH	REMARKS
1	Top	Walnut	1	24¼	47¾	
2	Top battens (end)	Walnut	1	2¼	23⅞	Miter to top ends, ⅜ in. from front edge.
4	Legs	Walnut	1⅞	1⅞	30	Mold and chamfer edges as shown.
2	Aprons	Walnut	1	5	43¼	40¾ in. between tenons
2	Aprons	Walnut	1	5	19¾	17¼ in. between tenons
2	Moldings	Walnut	1 1/16	1½	46⅝	Miter to frame.
2	Moldings	Walnut	1 1/16	1½	23⅛	Miter to frame.
2	Moldings	Walnut	5/16	⅝	45⅛	Miter to frame.
2	Moldings	Walnut	5/16	⅝	21⅝	Miter to frame.
6	Brackets	Walnut	7/16	4	4	Scroll saw to pattern.
10	Table-top fasteners or cleats	Oak	13/16	1⅛	4	

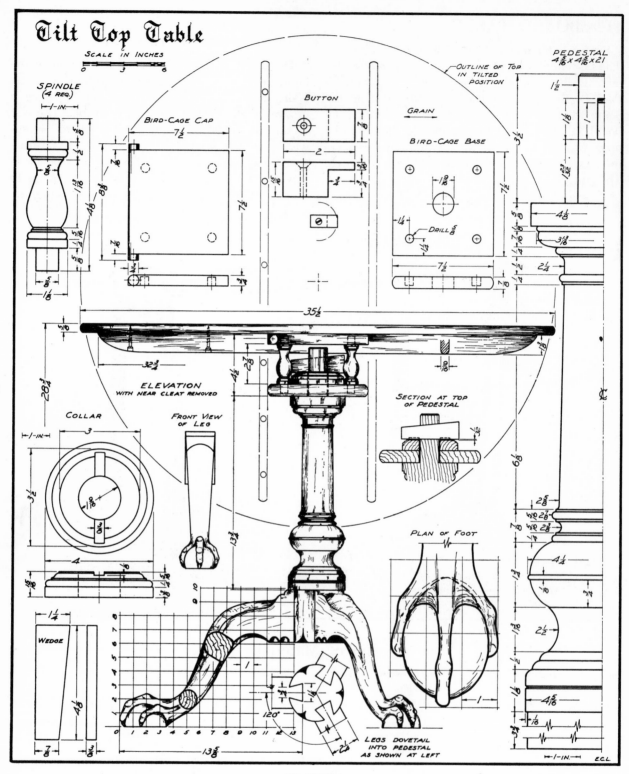

Tilt Top Table

PLATE 6

TILT-TOP TABLE

This Chippendale table of black walnut is similar to some of the Philadelphia tables seen in valued collections. It is well preserved, the wood soft and mellow, the color the rich deep brown that nature and age have given to walnut from the virgin forests of this country.

CONSTRUCTION NOTES

1. The large flat top of this table will be welcomed by craftsmen. The top revolves and is, in reality, a sort of Lazy Susan.

2. While the turned pedestal is in the lathe, the position of the dovetails for the legs may be marked, using the steady rest as a straightedge.

3. The slot in the upper part of the pedestal is laid out to be cut high enough to prevent binding the bird cage when the wedge is driven up tight.

4. Cut the dovetail pins on the three feet with accuracy. Mark the position of each on the column. Lay off the slots from the pins, using a sharp knife to get a close mark. Carefully cut the slots, trim them with a sharp chisel, and fit until a good joint has been assured. The pedestal was not flattened to take the legs but the legs were made to conform to the curvature of the turning. A metal spider screwed to the column and the legs will insure a much stronger job.

5. The line of the pedestal end between the legs is broken by a graceful notch that may be filed or carved in.

6. A ⅜-in. wide slot across the diameter of the collar is engaged by the key or wedge and thus the collar is prevented from turning when the top is rotated.

Bill of Materials

PIECES	ARTICLE	KIND OF WOOD	THICKNESS	WIDTH	LENGTH	REMARKS
1	Top	Walnut	⅝	35½	35½	Saw out to circle and shape edge.
1	Pedestal	Walnut	4⁵⁄₁₆	4⁵⁄₁₆	22	21 net; turn
3	Legs	Walnut	3	5	17	Cut to pattern.
2	Cleats	Walnut	⁹⁄₁₆	1⅜	32¾	
1	Bird-cage cap	Walnut	¾	7½	8⅜	Work dowels on ends.
1	Bird-cage base	Walnut	⅞	7½	7½	
4	Bird-cage spindles	Walnut	1⅛	1⅛	5	⅞ in. allowed for centers
1	Collar	Walnut	¹⁵⁄₁₆	4	4	Turn.
1	Wedge	Walnut	⅜	1¼	4⅛	
1	Button	Walnut	¹⁵⁄₁₆	⅞	2	

End Table

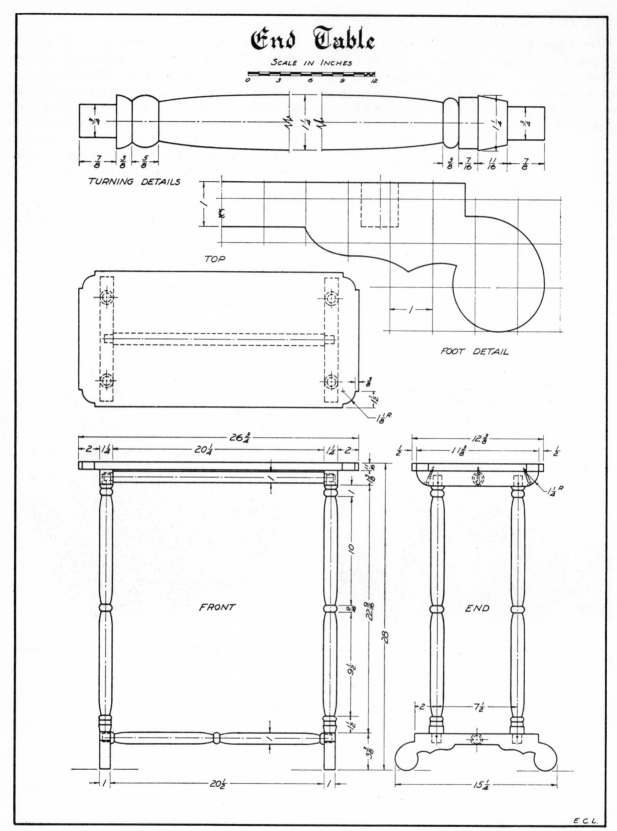

SCALE IN INCHES

TURNING DETAILS

TOP

FOOT DETAIL

FRONT

END

PLATE 7

E.C.L.

26

END TABLE

A type of table seen occasionally in the mountains of Virginia, it is something of an oddity but useful enough to have some amount of appeal. Some will like its rather primitive design, while for others the challenge will lie in the variations and improvements that come to the inventive mind.

CONSTRUCTION NOTES

1. Size the tenons carefully and guard the distances between them, because the table has not much strength other than in well-fitted tenons.

2. The top appears too narrow for the base, and, since the top is not the original one though known to bear the original shape, it might be made at least as wide as the feet. Such a change will give it more grace.

Bill of Materials

PIECES	ARTICLE	KIND OF WOOD	THICKNESS	WIDTH	LENGTH	REMARKS
1	Top	Walnut	$^{11}/_{16}$	$12\frac{3}{8}$	$26\frac{3}{4}$	
4	Legs	Walnut	$1\frac{1}{4}$	$1\frac{1}{4}$	$24\frac{5}{16}$	$22\frac{9}{16}$ in. between tenons
2	Top battens	Walnut	$1\frac{1}{4}$	$1\frac{3}{8}$	$11\frac{3}{8}$	
2	Feet	Walnut	1	$3\frac{3}{8}$	$15\frac{1}{4}$	
1	Top stretcher	Walnut	1	1	$22\frac{1}{4}$	$20\frac{1}{4}$ in. between tenons
1	Bottom stretcher	Walnut	1	1	22	$20\frac{1}{2}$ in. between tenons; $\frac{3}{4}$ in. into leg

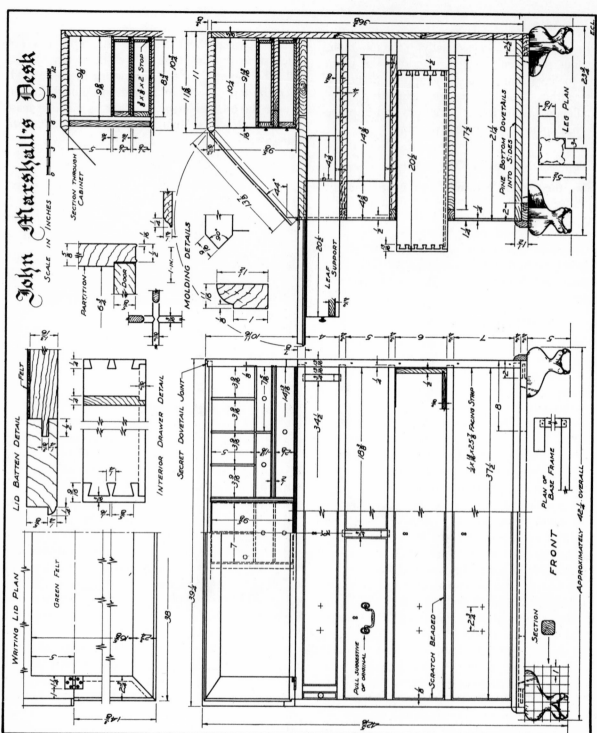

John Marshall's Desk

PLATE 8

JOHN MARSHALL'S DESK

The home of John Marshall, the great jurist, in Richmond, Virginia, has been made a shrine to American history by the Association for the Preservation of Virginia Antiquities. After some detective work in its effort to restore to the home its original furnishings, the association located Marshall's desk in New York.

The hardware shown on the piece is not original nor even the style of the original, and it is, furthermore, upside down. Outlines of the original plates and plugged holes show clearly that pulls similar to the one indicated on the drawing were used when the desk was made. The drawer fronts are solid crotch walnut whose beautiful swirling grain is a prominent feature of this handsome piece of furniture.

CONSTRUCTION NOTES

1. Every outward appearance indicates that secret dovetail joints were used to join the top to the ends. A half-hidden dovetail joint, though not as neat in appearance, is strong and attractive without being tedious to build.

2. Glue up the desk ends to form rectangles 21 by 36¾ in. Leave them rectangular while the desk is built up, waiting until the lid is to be fitted on before sawing them off for the slant top. The desk-top board must have its front edge beveled as shown before it is attached to the ends. Before cutting the ends off, mark them carefully, allowing for the lip on the lid. Saw them off with a handsaw, run a jack plane up the edges to smooth the cut, and bring the work down to the marked line.

3. Pine boards faced with 1¼-in. strips of walnut are dadoed into the desk ends to a depth of ¼ in., serving the purpose of drawer framing. These should be glued into the dadoes. The dadoes were cut through the entire width of the ends, but the joints were hidden by a ¼ by 1³⁄₁₆-in. facing strip of walnut glued and nailed up the front edges of the ends. A stopped dado would have made a neater job. If facing strips are used, drawer shelves will have to be notched to come flush with them. If stopped dado joints are to replace facing strips, increase the width of the desk ends ¼ in. These joints have almost no strength to withstand a pulling apart force. The dovetail joints on the top and bottom hold the two ends together.

4. Pigeonhole partitions are dadoed into the ends and the top, but are V-notched into each other.

5. With a hand router plane, recess the writing shelf ¹⁄₁₆ in. as shown, if a felt writing area is intended. Do the work in strips, so that the plane will have a bearing surface. Remove the strips with a chisel or bullnose plane working across the grain. As shown in a detail, the recess is made on the writing lid by a difference of ¹⁄₁₆ in. in thickness between the lid proper and its three surrounding battens. If the surface is not to be felt covered, set the lid hinges farther in from the lid ends than on the model. A spline, ³⁄₁₆ by ½ in., was worked on the original desk lid and out of center as shown; but tenons cut and fitted into hidden mortises along the end battens are stronger. Because mortise-and-tenon joints are preferred on end battens, the material bill has been so made. The front batten should be splined in the miters but butt jointed across the writing-lid edge.

6. A stop pin made of a short length of ³⁄₈-in. dowel is put on the inside surface of each pull-out lid support 4⅞ in. from the back end of the support, allowing 11 in. to support the writing lid. Do not glue these pins into the holes.

7. For the short ball and claw feet, use pieces of stock 3 by 3 in. to which 2½-in. wide ears are glued. These may be glued on before or after the rest of the foot has been worked.

8. A few large screws driven into the feet from the frame above will, with glue, make them secure. Another method would mortise them into the pine frame and wedge the mortise.

Bill of Materials

PIECES	ARTICLE	KIND OF WOOD	THICKNESS	WIDTH	LENGTH	REMARKS
1	Top	Walnut	13/16	11 5/16	39 1/4	37 1/2 in. between dovetails
2	Ends	Walnut	13/16	21	36 3/4	Rabbet back inside edges 1/2 by 5/8 for backing.
2	End facing strips	Walnut	1/4	13/16	25 7/8	
1	Bottom	Pine	3/4	20 5/8	38 3/4	37 1/2 in. between dovetails
1	Writing shelf	Walnut	7/8	11 7/8	38	Dado 1/4 in. into ends.
1	Writing-shelf back	Pine	7/8	8 3/4	38	Glue to edge of walnut shelf and dado as above.
3	Drawer shelves	Pine	3/4	17 1/2	38	Dado 1/4 in. into ends.
3	Facing strips	Walnut	3/4	1 1/4	38	Glue to front edge of shelves above.
2	Drawer stiles	Walnut	3/4	4 3/8	4 1/2	4 in. between shoulders
1	Drawer stile	Walnut	3/4	4 3/8	5 1/2	5 in. between shoulders
3	Drawer guides	Pine	3/4	7/8	14 3/8	Dado 1/4 in. into drawer shelves.
1	Backing	Pine	5/8	36 3/8	38 1/2	Allow extra width for 1/2-in. ship-lap joints.
1	Base-frame front	Pine	3/4	2	39 1/4	
2	Base-frame sides	Pine	3/4	2	17 3/4	15 3/4 in. between tenons
2	Base-frame backs	Pine	3/4	2 1/2	8	
1	Base molding	Walnut	11/16	1 1/2	41	Miter and glue to base frame.
2	Base moldings	Walnut	11/16	1 1/2	21	Miter and glue to base frame.
4	Legs	Walnut	5 1/2	5 1/2	5	
1	Writing lid	Walnut	13/16	11 5/8	35	32 1/2 in. between tenons. Make 7/8 in. thick if lid is not to be felt covered.
1	Writing-lid batten	Walnut	7/8	2 3/4	38	
2	Writing-lid battens	Walnut	7/8	2 3/4	14 3/8	
2	Lid supports	Walnut	3/4	3 15/16	20 1/2	
	Drawers					
1	Front	Walnut	13/16	3 15/16	34 7/16	
2	Fronts	Walnut	13/16	4 15/16	18 5/16	
1	Front	Walnut	13/16	5 15/16	37 7/16	
1	Front	Walnut	13/16	6 15/16	37 7/16	
2	Sides	Pine	1/2	3 15/16	20 1/4	
4	Sides	Pine	1/2	4 15/16	20 1/4	
2	Sides	Pine	1/2	5 15/16	20 1/4	
2	Sides	Pine	1/2	6 15/16	20 1/4	
1	Back	Pine	1/2	3 7/16	34 7/16	
2	Backs	Pine	1/2	4 7/16	18 5/16	
1	Back	Pine	1/2	5 7/16	37 7/16	
1	Back	Pine	1/2	6 7/16	37 7/16	
1	Bottom	Pine	3/8	20	33 15/16	1/4 by 1/4-in. grooves into sides and front
2	Bottoms	Pine	3/8	20	17 13/16	
2	Bottoms	Pine	3/8	20	36 15/16	
	Interior of Desk					
1	Bottom	Walnut	1/4	10 3/4	37 1/2	
2	Cabinet stiles	Walnut	5/8	10 1/4	9 7/8	1/8-in. stop dado top and bottom. Rabbet 1/8 by 5/8 in. for door. Mold front edge as shown.
1	Cabinet door	Walnut	5/8	7	9 9/16	
2	Drawer shelves	Pine	1/2	8 1/4	15 1/16	
2	Drawer-shelf facings	Walnut	1/2	2	15 1/16	Glue to shelves above and dado 1/8 in. into sides.
2	Pigeonhole shelves	Walnut	3/16	10 1/4	15 1/16	Stop dado 1/8 in. into ends.
2	Drawer stiles	Walnut	3/16	10 1/4	2	V-notch 1/16 in. into shelves.
6	Partitions	Walnut	3/16	10 1/4	5 3/16	1/16-in. V notch into shelves; 1/8-in. stop dado into top
1	Cabinet partition	Walnut	3/16	9 1/8	5 3/16	1/16-in. V notch into shelves; 1/8-in. stop dado into top
2	Cabinet shelves	Walnut	3/16	9 1/8	7	Stop dado 1/8 in. into stiles.

PIECES	ARTICLE	KIND OF WOOD	THICKNESS	WIDTH	LENGTH	REMARKS
2	Cabinet-drawer fronts	Walnut	9/16	2 1/16	6 11/16	
4	Cabinet-drawer sides	Pine	1/4	2 1/16	8 9/16	
2	Cabinet-drawer backs	Pine	1/4	2 1/16	6 11/16	
2	Cabinet-drawer bottoms	Pine	3/16	8 7/16	6 7/16	
	Drawers					
4	Fronts	Walnut	9/16	1 3/4	7 1/4	
2	Fronts	Walnut	9/16	2 1/16	14 3/4	
8	Sides	Pine	1/4	1 3/4	9 5/8	
4	Sides	Pine	1/4	2 1/16	9 5/8	
4	Backs	Pine	1/4	1 3/4	7 1/4	
2	Backs	Pine	1/4	2 1/16	14 3/4	
4	Bottoms	Pine	3/16	9 1/2	7	
2	Bottoms	Pine	3/16	9 1/2	14 1/2	
1	Stop	Pine	3/8	3/8	36	Cut into 2-in. lengths, two to each drawer.

Hardware: 8 drawer pulls, 2¾ in. (Wm. Ball, No. 35); 5 drawer or till locks, 1⅛ in. selvedge to key pin; 1 desk-lid lock; 6 brass thread escutcheons; 9 brass knobs, 7/16 in. diameter; 2 brass desk hinges, 1¼ in. long; 2 narrow butt brass hinges, 1 in. long; 1 piece green felt, 16½ by 33½; 2 brass knobs, ⅝-in. diameter

Secret dovetail joint

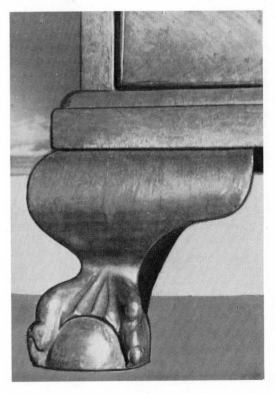

Ball and claw foot of desk

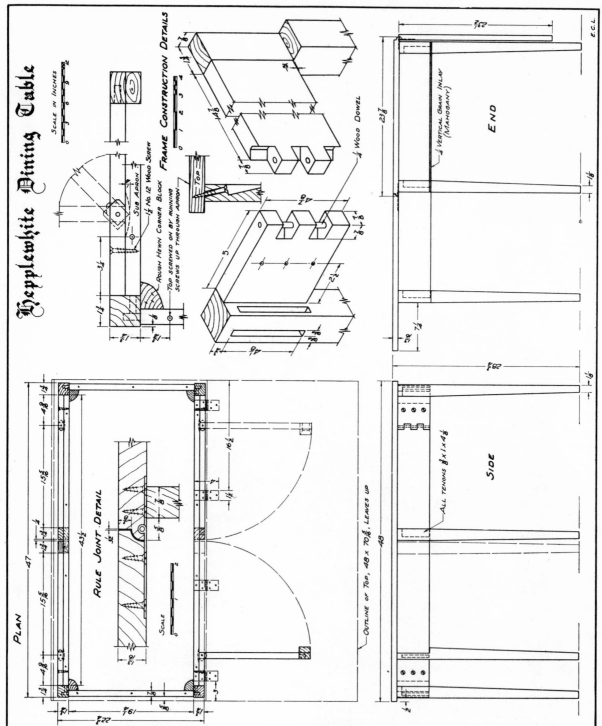

Hepplewhite Dining Table

FRAME CONSTRUCTION DETAILS

RULE JOINT DETAIL

PLAN

END

SIDE

PLATE 9

32

HEPPLEWHITE DINING TABLE

This beautiful American-made Hepplewhite table in three parts is a good example of one of the most popular table designs in this country. With its two half-circle ends (next article) against the wall on either side of a large doorway in an old Southern home, its center section was used, with leaves down, to seat two, or, with leaves up, to accommodate up to eight diners. The end tables were used to increase the number to twelve persons.

It is estimated to be one hundred and seventy-five years old, and is made of very dense red mahogany. Each top is a single board. The side aprons are yellow pine.

Hinged legs, set as on this table, open out to support the corners of the drop leaves.

CONSTRUCTION NOTES

1. Swinging legs are tapered on three sides, only the outside side is left straight.

2. Procedure for hinging leaves to a fixed top:

a) Spread out the top and both leaves upside down on a suitably smooth work surface — two nice straight 2 by 4's six feet long, supported by sawhorses, makes a good rig.

b) Line up the ends, and clamp all three sections together with strips of paper totaling $\frac{1}{32}$ in. thick in the rule joints for clearance. Apply hinges.

c) Fasten the table frame to the center top.

Bill of Materials

PIECES	ARTICLE	KIND OF WOOD	THICKNESS	WIDTH	LENGTH	REMARKS
1	Top	Mahogany	$1\frac{3}{16}$	$23\frac{7}{8}$	48	
2	Leaves	Mahogany	$1\frac{3}{16}$	$23\frac{1}{2}$	48	
8	Legs	Mahogany	$1\frac{3}{4}$	$1\frac{3}{4}$	$27\frac{15}{16}$	
2	Aprons, side	Yellow pine	$\frac{7}{8}$	$4\frac{7}{8}$	$45\frac{1}{2}$	$43\frac{1}{2}$ in. between tenons
2	Aprons, end	Mahogany	$\frac{7}{8}$	$4\frac{7}{8}$	$21\frac{1}{4}$	$19\frac{1}{4}$ in. between tenons
4	Hinge leaves, fixed	Mahogany	$\frac{7}{8}$	$4\frac{7}{8}$	5	
4	Hinge leaves, free	Mahogany	$\frac{7}{8}$	$4\frac{7}{8}$	$16\frac{3}{4}$	1-in. tenon on one end
4	Corner blocks	Yellow pine	$1\frac{1}{2}$	$1\frac{1}{2}$	$4\frac{7}{8}$	Rough hewn to shape on the back.

$1\frac{1}{2}$ yds. $\frac{1}{20}$ by $\frac{1}{4}$ mahogany vertical-grain inlay band

Hardware: 8 table hinges, $1\frac{1}{2}$ in.; $\frac{1}{4}$ by 20 wood dowel for hinge pins

33

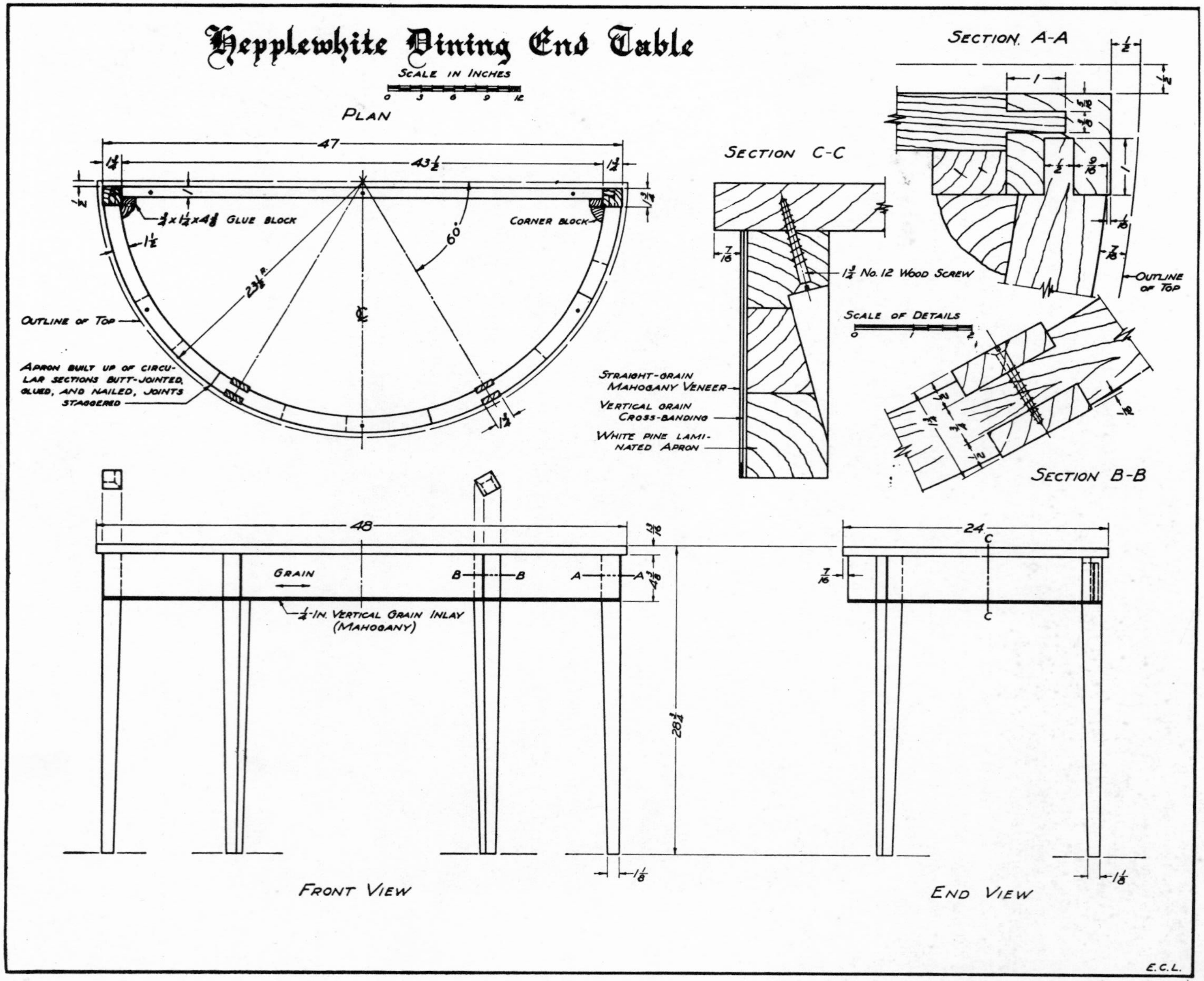

Hepplewhite Dining End Table

SECTION A-A

OUTLINE OF TOP

SECTION C-C

1½ No. 12 WOOD SCREW

SECTION B-B

SCALE OF DETAILS

Straight-Grain Mahogany Veneer
Vertical Grain Cross-Banding
White Pine Laminated Apron

PLAN

SCALE IN INCHES

CORNER BLOCK

½×1½×4½ GLUE BLOCK

43½

47

23½

6

OUTLINE OF TOP

Apron built up of circular sections butt-jointed, glued, and nailed, joints staggered

FRONT VIEW

GRAIN

½-IN VERTICAL GRAIN INLAY (MAHOGANY)

48

END VIEW

24

28½

E.C.L.

PLATE 10

34

HEPPLEWHITE DINING END TABLE

A pair of these semicircular end tables accompany the Hepplewhite drop-leaf table described on preceding pages. The ¼-in. band of inlay around the bottom of the circular aprons is so near the color of the rest of the table as to be indistinguishable at a distance.

CONSTRUCTION NOTES

1. Make a full-sized pattern of the semicircular apron on paper or plywood but do not cut it out. Make another pattern on the same radii but with a circumferential length of one fourth that of the full one. Cut out this pattern and mark off enough short arcs to make the laminated apron, when butted end to end in layers with joints staggered. A smoother job often results when the apron is made ¼ in. thicker than required, so that, after laminating, it can be band-sawed or planed down to the net size.

2. White pine is a stable wood for a built-up table apron to be veneered. The bill has the pieces ½ in. thick. Glue the pieces together end to end and edge to edge, using the full-size pattern as guide. If finishing nails are driven through the centers of the layers as they are built up, no clamping will be necessary. Do not drive nails where tenons must be cut with saws.

3. Crossbanding and face veneer may be put on at the same time, but some preparation must be made:

   a) Pieces of crossbanding have been butt jointed and taped to make pieces that reach from tenon space to tenon space.

   b) Pieces of face veneer have been cut the proper width and length to correspond.

   c) Veneer is tacked in place with small nails (½-in., No. 20) until clamps and blocks can be arranged and prevent slippage when pressure is applied.

   d) Clamps and heavy felt-covered blocks, cut to correct radius, and paper to go between face veneer and clamping blocks must be at hand.

   e) A sufficient quantity of glue ready to use with a 2-in. brush. The new urea-resin glues give the craftsman time to apply his clamps before setting up. Use plenty of glue. Glue is cheaper than a starved joint.

4. See that pressure is on over the entire surface, once the clamps have been put on; otherwise, blisters are likely to show up.

5. The apron of the end tables is 4⅜ in. wide; whereas, those of the center section are 4⅞ in. All other measurements indicate that these three tables are a set.

Bill of Materials (Build Two)

PIECES	ARTICLE	KIND OF WOOD	THICKNESS	WIDTH	LENGTH	REMARKS
2	Tops	Mahogany	$1\frac{3}{16}$	24	48	Cut to half circles
8	Legs	Mahogany	$1\frac{3}{4}$	$1\frac{3}{4}$	$27^{15}\!/_{16}$	
2	Back aprons	Yellow pine	1	$4\frac{5}{8}$	$45\frac{1}{2}$	43½ in. between tenons
2	Built-up-circular aprons	White pine	$1\frac{1}{2}$	$4\frac{3}{8}$		Radius of 23½ in., 180 deg., crossband with vertical-grained veneer, and then veneer with straight-grained mahogany.
4	Glue blocks	White pine	¾	$1\frac{1}{4}$	$4\frac{3}{8}$	
4	Corner blocks	White pine	$1\frac{1}{2}$	$1\frac{1}{2}$	$4\frac{3}{8}$	Rough hewn to shape.

Straight-grained mahogany veneer as needed
4½ yds. ¹⁄₂₀ by ¼ mahogany vertical-grained inlay band

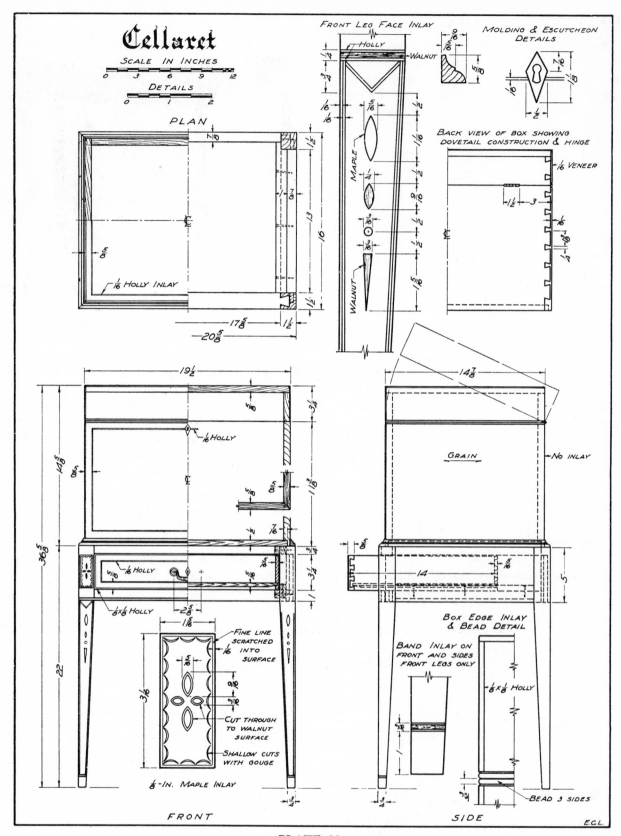

Cellaret

SCALE IN INCHES

0   3   6   9   12

DETAILS

0   1   2

PLAN

FRONT LEG FACE INLAY

MOLDING & ESCUTCHEON
DETAILS

BACK VIEW OF BOX SHOWING
DOVETAIL CONSTRUCTION & HINGE

GRAIN

NO INLAY

FINE LINE
SCRATCHED
INTO
SURFACE

CUT THROUGH
TO WALNUT
SURFACE

SHALLOW CUTS
WITH GOUGE

BOX EDGE INLAY
& BEAD DETAIL

BAND INLAY ON
FRONT AND SIDES
FRONT LEGS ONLY

BEAD 3 SIDES

FRONT

SIDE

E.C.L.

PLATE 11

CELLARET

No piece of furniture is more typical of the old South than the cellaret where it occupied a place of prominence in the dining room. Many and varied examples have come down to us, representing most of the popular periods of furniture, but those most popular gracefully embodied the spirits of Chippendale and Hepplewhite. It was a storage place for liquors, usually divided into twelve sections for bottles and the various condiments — nutmeg, mace, cloves, sugar — and so on, used in mixing drinks. A drawer in the frame beneath held cutlery. Frequently a slide for mixing either replaced or was in addition to the drawer. Occasionally one was found with a slate top for mixing.

This cellaret has no partitions for bottles nor is there a lock on the drawer. The inlaid escutcheon is a disguise.

The over-all design of the cellaret lends itself to our imaginations for other uses than the storage of liquors.

CONSTRUCTION NOTES

1. No sign of its top ever having expanded or contracted was visible to mar the flush joints back and front on the case lid. Nonetheless, the use of walnut-faced plywood for this member is recommended. We rarely have as fine lumber as craftsmen two hundreds years ago; just as rarely do we have proper humidity conditions in our homes. If plywood is to be used, it should be set in rabbets all around the top whose cheek cuts are $\frac{1}{8}$ in. from the lid edges. Such construction will entail changing the materials list, so that all four lid sides will be $\frac{5}{8}$ by $3\frac{1}{4}$ in. in cross section. And this, in turn, suggests

Bill of Materials

PIECES	ARTICLE	KIND OF WOOD	THICKNESS	WIDTH	LENGTH	REMARKS
	Case					
1	Front	Walnut	$\frac{5}{8}$	$11\frac{3}{8}$	$19\frac{1}{2}$	
2	Sides	Walnut	$\frac{5}{8}$	$11\frac{3}{8}$	$14\frac{7}{8}$	
1	Back	White pine	$\frac{5}{8}$	$11\frac{3}{8}$	$19\frac{3}{8}$	
1	Bottom	White pine	$\frac{1}{2}$	$14\frac{1}{2}$	$19\frac{1}{8}$	
1	Lid top	Walnut	$\frac{5}{8}$	$14\frac{13}{16}$	$19\frac{3}{8}$	
1	Lid front	Walnut	$\frac{5}{8}$	$2\frac{5}{8}$	$19\frac{3}{8}$	
2	Lid sides	Walnut	$\frac{9}{16}$	$2\frac{5}{8}$	$14\frac{13}{16}$	
1	Lid back	White pine	$\frac{5}{8}$	$2\frac{5}{8}$	$19\frac{3}{8}$	
2	Lid sides veneer	Walnut	$\frac{1}{16}$	$3\frac{1}{4}$	$14\frac{7}{8}$	
	Frame					
4	Legs	Walnut	$1\frac{1}{2}$	$1\frac{1}{2}$	22	
1	Drawer rail	Walnut	$\frac{3}{4}$	$1\frac{1}{2}$	$19\frac{5}{8}$	$17\frac{5}{8}$ in. between dovetails
1	Drawer rail	Walnut	1	$1\frac{1}{2}$	$19\frac{5}{8}$	$17\frac{5}{8}$ in. between tenons
2	Sides	Walnut	$\frac{7}{8}$	5	15	13 in. between tenons
1	Back	Yellow pine	$\frac{7}{8}$	5	$19\frac{5}{8}$	$17\frac{5}{8}$ in. between tenons
2	Moldings	Walnut	$\frac{9}{16}$	$\frac{5}{8}$	$21\frac{3}{4}$	Miter and nail to frame top edge.
2	Moldings	Walnut	$\frac{9}{16}$	$\frac{5}{8}$	$17\frac{1}{8}$	Miter and nail to frame top edge.
4	Drawer runners	Yellow pine	$\frac{3}{4}$	1	$13\frac{5}{8}$	Cut out around back legs; nail and glue to sides.
2	Drawer guides	Yellow pine	$\frac{1}{2}$	$\frac{5}{8}$	13	
	Drawer					
1	Front	Walnut	$\frac{5}{8}$	$3\frac{3}{16}$	$17\frac{9}{16}$	
2	Sides	Yellow pine	$\frac{5}{16}$	$3\frac{3}{16}$	$13\frac{9}{16}$	
1	Back	Yellow pine	$\frac{5}{16}$	$2\frac{9}{16}$	$17\frac{9}{16}$	
1	Bottom	White pine	$\frac{5}{16}$	$13\frac{5}{8}$	$17\frac{5}{16}$	
2	Leg-panel inlay	Maple	$\frac{1}{8}$	$1\frac{5}{16}$	$3\frac{1}{16}$	Carve as detailed.

4 yds. $\frac{1}{8}$ by $\frac{1}{8}$ holly inlay
1 yd. $\frac{1}{20}$ by $\frac{1}{4}$ holly, walnut, holly band inlay
1 yd. $\frac{1}{20}$ by $\frac{3}{16}$ holly, walnut, holly band inlay
5 yds. $\frac{1}{20}$ by $\frac{1}{16}$ holly line inlay

Hardware: 1 chest lock; 1 pr. butt hinges — $1\frac{1}{2}$ in.; 1 drawer pull (Ball, No. 35, $2\frac{1}{2}$-in. bore)

making the entire case in one piece, later sawing off the upper 3¼-in. portion to form a lid that will be square with the bottom section. It is obvious that the two pieces of horizontally grained ¹⁄₁₆-in. thick veneer were applied to the original lid sides to hide the end grain of the top.

2. Handily, the lines of ⅛ by ⅛-in. holly conceal all veneer and miter joints on the case. A scratch stock will bead the edges of the case as shown.

3. It is rare to find inlay as near the edge as it is on the face of these legs, but it adds to the impression of delicacy. No inlay appears on the back legs, and the line along the bottom drawer rail does not carry around and along the sides as we might expect.

4. Back-of-case dovetails cut to within ¹⁄₁₆ in. of the side surface. The idea of the builder seems to have been that of further disguising the veneer glued to the sides of the lid.

5. Notice the incised petals on the maple medallion that is inlaid into the front legs. Some such shallow carved places were filled with whiting, allowed to harden, and then sanded smooth, becoming like bone with age. Often the plastic material was colored with pigments. There is no indication, however, that these depressions were ever filled with anything.

CORNER CUPBOARD

Corner cupboards have had an almost universal appeal in the South for two hundred years. They were much used in kitchens as well as in dining rooms, and occasionally were found stocked with books and other paraphernalia in a sitting room. Their sizes and styles vary, so that it is not common to find two alike. The one selected for this collection is of a good size, neither too small nor too large. It has a drawer and that other useful feature, large panes of glass in a single door. It isn't enough that a corner cupboard store family china and glassware; it must display it for the pleasure it gives to all in the house. Two doors have certain advantages, but they necessitate two additional stiles down the center front where they cut off the view. Another nice thing about this old cupboard, copied in the Valley of Virginia, is that a stock-size window glass was used.

CONSTRUCTION NOTES

1. First build the frame. Into this will fit doors and drawer. It will help to groove all four stiles for splines before assembling the frame. Make special blocks to use under the clamps, in order not to bruise the miter when clamping up the frame.

2. Clamping blocks like those shown in the sketch will aid greatly in the work of joining the frame to the outside stiles.

3. The doors of this old cupboard present a construction oddity in that the stiles mortise into the rails rather than the rails into the stiles. Individuality thrived at the time of its building. Work the

Bill of Materials

PIECES	ARTICLE	KIND OF WOOD	THICKNESS	WIDTH	LENGTH	REMARKS
2	Outside stiles	Walnut	$^{15}/_{16}$	$3\frac{3}{4}$	84	
2	Frame stiles	Walnut	$^{15}/_{16}$	$2\frac{7}{8}$	84	
2	Splines	Walnut	$\frac{3}{8}$	$\frac{3}{4}$	84	
1	Frame top rail	Walnut	$^{15}/_{16}$	$3\frac{1}{4}$	$29\frac{3}{4}$	$27\frac{3}{4}$ in. between tenons
3	Frame center and bottom rails	Walnut	$^{15}/_{16}$	$2\frac{1}{4}$	$29\frac{3}{4}$	$27\frac{3}{4}$ in. between tenons
2	Drawer stiles	Walnut	$^{15}/_{16}$	$3\frac{1}{2}$	$5\frac{1}{2}$	$4\frac{1}{2}$ in. between tenons
1	Top molding	Walnut	$^{15}/_{16}$	$3\frac{1}{4}$	48	Miter around finished frame.
1	Center backpiece	Poplar	$\frac{3}{4}$	$5\frac{3}{8}$	$80\frac{3}{4}$	
1	Backing	Poplar	$\frac{1}{2}$	48	$80\frac{3}{4}$	Allow extra width for lap joints — cut out to make feet.
4	Top, center, bottom shelves	Poplar	$\frac{3}{4}$	18	$37\frac{3}{16}$	Dado $\frac{1}{4}$ in. deep into center backpiece and outside stiles.
3	Shelves	Poplar	$\frac{5}{8}$	18	$37\frac{3}{16}$	
1	Back foot brace	Poplar	2	3	$3\frac{3}{4}$	
	Drawer					
1	Front	Walnut	$^{15}/_{16}$	$4\frac{7}{16}$	$20\frac{11}{16}$	
1	Back	Poplar	$\frac{5}{8}$	$3\frac{13}{16}$	$20\frac{11}{16}$	
2	Sides	Poplar	$\frac{1}{2}$	$4\frac{7}{16}$	$10\frac{5}{16}$	
1	Bottom	Poplar	$\frac{1}{4}$	$9\frac{7}{8}$	$20\frac{3}{16}$	
2	Drawer runners	Poplar	$\frac{3}{4}$	$1\frac{3}{4}$	$11\frac{1}{4}$	$\frac{3}{8}$-in. tenon on one end; miter other end to fit case.
2	Drawer guides	Poplar	$\frac{3}{4}$	1	10	Glue and nail to runners.
2	Door stiles	Walnut	$^{15}/_{16}$	$1\frac{3}{4}$	$43\frac{1}{2}$	$40\frac{15}{16}$ in. between tenons
2	Door rails	Walnut	$^{15}/_{16}$	$1\frac{3}{4}$	$27\frac{3}{4}$	
3	Mullions	Walnut	$^{15}/_{16}$	$\frac{5}{8}$	$27\frac{7}{8}$	$24\frac{11}{16}$ in. between tenons; cope mold to fit shoulders.
8	Mullions	Walnut	$^{15}/_{16}$	$\frac{5}{8}$	$10\frac{9}{32}$	$9\frac{21}{32}$ in. between tenons; cope mold to fit shoulders.
4	Door stiles	Walnut	$^{15}/_{16}$	$1\frac{3}{4}$	$21\frac{5}{8}$	$19\frac{1}{8}$ in. between tenons; cope mold to fit shoulders.
4	Door rails	Walnut	$^{15}/_{16}$	2	$18\frac{7}{8}$	
2	Door panels	Walnut	$\frac{3}{8}$	$10\frac{7}{8}$	$19\frac{3}{16}$	$\frac{1}{8}$-in. play horizontally; $\frac{1}{16}$-in. vertically
1	Door button	Walnut	$\frac{5}{8}$	$\frac{3}{4}$	$1\frac{1}{4}$	

Hardware: 6 broad butt brass hinges, $1\frac{1}{2}$ in.; 2 cupboard turns, $1\frac{1}{4}$ in. (Ball, No. 350); 2 drawer pulls (Ball, No. 24), $2\frac{1}{4}$ in.; 12 window glass 8 by 10

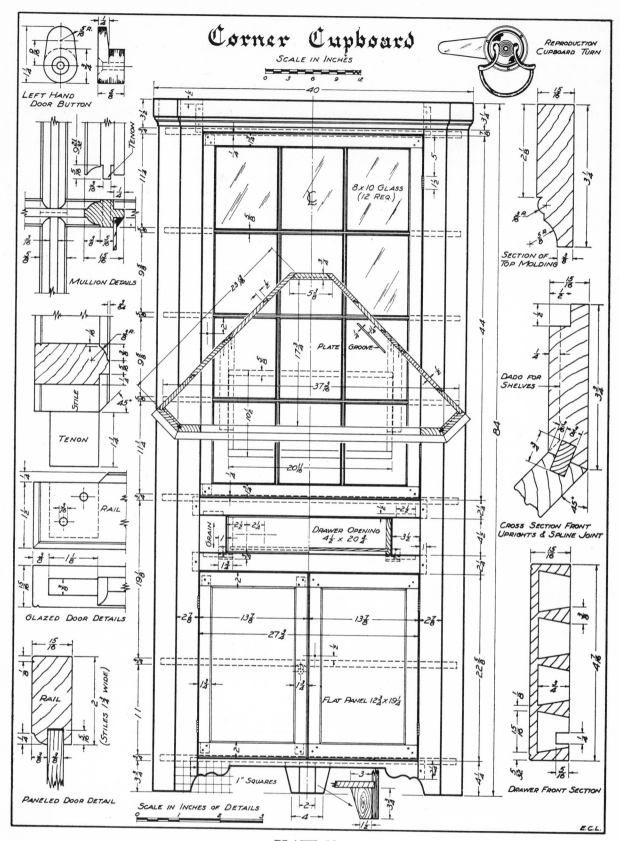

Corner Cupboard

SCALE IN INCHES

LEFT HAND DOOR BUTTON

MULLION DETAILS

STILE

TENON

RAIL

GLAZED DOOR DETAILS

RAIL

(STILES 1¾ WIDE)

PANELED DOOR DETAIL

SCALE IN INCHES OF DETAILS

8x10 GLASS (12 REQ.)

PLATE GROOVE

DRAWER OPENING 4½ x 20¼

GRAIN

FLAT PANEL 12¾ x 19¼

1" SQUARES

REPRODUCTION CUPBOARD TURN

SECTION OF TOP MOLDING

DADO FOR SHELVES

CROSS SECTION FRONT UPRIGHTS & SPLINE JOINT

DRAWER FRONT SECTION

E.C.L.

PLATE 12

bead around all doors after they have been fitted to openings.

4. Backing is nailed into the rabbeted outside stiles and to the shelves from top to bottom. It is random-width poplar boards with a ship-lap joint worked on the edges.

5. Note that spacing of top, center, and bottom shelves provide door stops.

6. Before swinging the upper door, determine the way it should open for the space it will occupy to obviate a conflict with a room door. Whether or not the person who will use the cupboard most is right- or left-handed may make a difference.

7. The addition of another molding to give more flare to the top and the use of brass H hinges (in place of butt hinges) will dress up the piece, but is offered merely as a suggestion. Another suggestion is that a wardrobe or mortise cabinet-door lock be used on the bottom doors instead of a cupboard turn to keep little children away from fragile things.

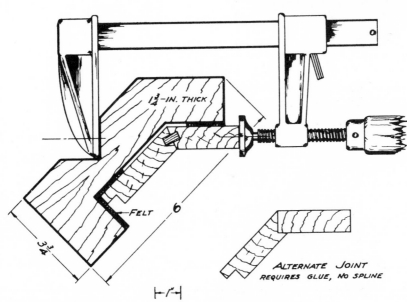

Suggested clamping block

41

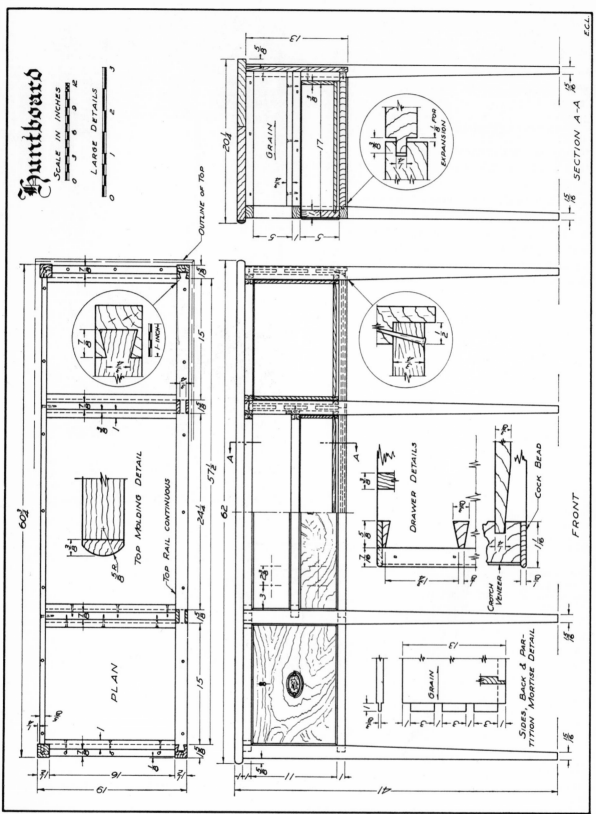

Huntboard

SCALE IN INCHES

LARGE DETAILS

SECTION A-A

GRAIN

FOR EXPANSION

OUTLINE OF TOP

TOP MOLDING DETAIL

TOP RAIL CONTINUOUS

PLAN

DRAWER DETAILS

CROTCH VENEER

COCK BEAD

FRONT

GRAIN

SIDES, BACK & PAR-
TITION MORTISE DETAIL

PLATE 13

42

HUNTBOARD

The George Hepplewhite style of huntboard is familiar in the South. They usually are plainer than large sideboards, and, because of their size, are better suited to small homes.

CONSTRUCTION NOTES

1. The legs are not square.

2. Inside front legs taper on three sides, others on inside edges.

3. Face wood usually was veneered as shown on these drawer fronts. Crossbanding is used under the face veneer, as stated elsewhere. Crossbanding is valuable with highly figured veneers. It can be any straight-grained veneer whose grain is planted at right angles to the face veneer.

4. The bottom is tongue-grooved into the drawer rails in front; cut out around the posts; rabbeted and nailed into the ends; and butt jointed and nailed to the back.

5. The outside drawers are deep and will need additional clearance. The fronts and sides should have $\frac{1}{16}$-in. allowance, in accordance with the original.

Bill of Materials

PIECES	ARTICLE	KIND OF WOOD	THICKNESS	WIDTH	LENGTH	REMARKS
1	Top	Walnut	1	19⅞	61¼	
6	Legs	Walnut	1½	1⅝	40	
1	Drawer rail	Walnut	1	1⅝	59¼	57½ in. between dovetails
2	Center-drawer rails	Walnut	1	1⅝	25¾	24¼ in. between tenons
2	Outside-drawer rails	Walnut	1	1⅝	16½	15 in. between tenons
2	Ends	Walnut	⅞	13	18	16 in. between tenons
2	Partitions	Yellow pine	⅞	12	17	1-in. tenon one end
1	Back	Yellow pine	⅝	13	59½	57½ in. between tenons
1	Bottom	Yellow pine	¾	16⅞	59¾	Groove into bottom-drawer rails; rabbet into ends.
8	Drawer runners	Yellow pine	1	1	16⅝	
2	Drawer guides	Yellow pine	⅝	¾	16⅝	
6	Drawer guides	Yellow pine	⅜	¾	16⅝	
1	Top molding	Walnut	⅜	1	62	Miter to top.
2	Top moldings	Walnut	⅜	1	20¼	Miter to top.
	Drawers					
2	Fronts	Walnut	15⁄16	10 11⁄16	14 15⁄16	1⁄16-in. vertical play allowed; ⅛ in. might be better in many sections.
2	Fronts	Walnut	15⁄16	4 11⁄16	24 3⁄16	
4	Sides	Pine	⅜	10⅞	16⅝	
4	Sides	Pine	⅜	4⅞	16⅝	
2	Backs	Pine	⅜	10⅛	14 15⁄16	
2	Backs	Pine	⅜	4⅛	24 3⁄16	
2	Bottoms	Pine	⅜	16 5⁄16	14 9⁄16	
2	Bottoms	Pine	⅜	16 5⁄16	23 13⁄16	
4	Astragals	Walnut	⅛	1 1⁄16	15	
4	Astragals	Walnut	⅛	1 1⁄16	24¼	Miter around drawers.
6	Astragals	Walnut	⅛	7⁄16	12	

Crotch veneer to cover all drawer fronts — fronts are not matched veneer.
Crossbanding for above

Hardware: 6 drawer pulls (Ball, No. 3203, 2¼-in. bore); 4 till locks; 4 thread escutcheons

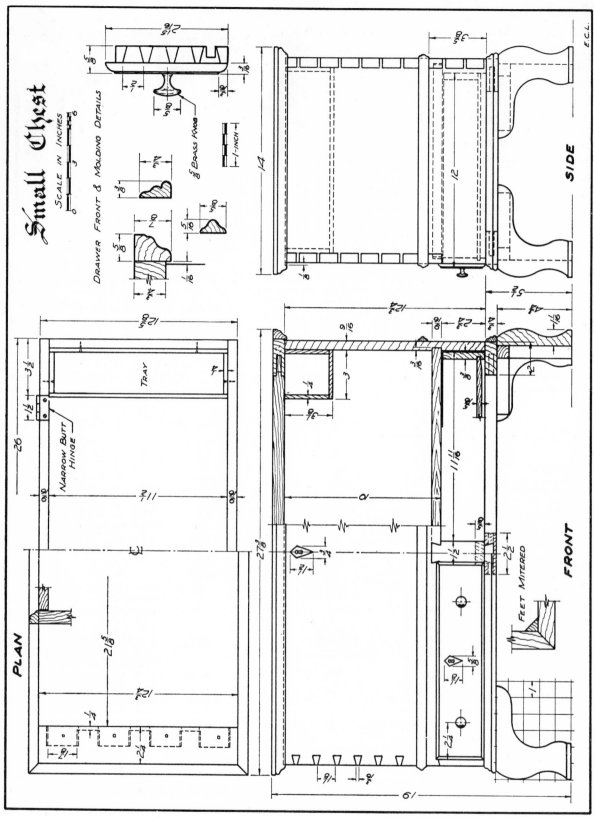

Small Chest

SCALE IN INCHES

DRAWER FRONT & MOLDING DETAILS

PLAN

TRAY

FRONT

SIDE

FEET MITERED

NARROW BUTT HINGE

PLATE 14

E.C.L.

44

SMALL CHEST

In early times, cane sugar and many of the other condiments and spices were scarce and expensive. So rare a treat and so tempting were they that steps had to be taken to safeguard against their misappropriation. It is said that the per capita consumption of cane sugar in the early eighteen hundreds was only about a pound each year. When we compare this with today's figure of a hundred times that amount we begin to understand how very good a small lump of sugar broken from the family loaf tasted to young and old alike. The stuff simply had to be kept under lock and key, and so it was that small chests that could be locked came into homes to fill a real need.

We are led to believe that this is one of the old sugar chests of that day. Not only its diminutive size but the presence of locks on all openings and even its fixed tray would so indicate its early use. As sugar and spices generally became more plentiful, it is logical that the lock boxes for such things would

fall into disuse and gradually disappear. They are harder to find now than sugar was once.

The one shown here was copied in Lexington, Virginia, where its imaginative owner uses it in front of a sofa as a sort of coffee table, sewing box, and repository for such things as snapshots and magazines. Its lines are well suited for scaling up to the size of a blanket chest with or without drawers.

CONSTRUCTION NOTES

1. The case, with its through dovetail corners, is made like the old six board chests, except that the bottom is a false one, leaving room below for the drawers. Base frame and legs or feet are glued and nailed to the chest. The base molding serves to hide the construction.

2. Groove the chest back and rabbet the chest front each $5/16$ in. deep to allow for expansion and contraction of a solid wood bottom. If a plywood

Bill of Materials

PIECES	ARTICLE	KIND OF WOOD	THICKNESS	WIDTH	LENGTH	REMARKS
1	Top	Walnut	$3/4$	$12\frac{3}{4}$	$24\frac{1}{8}$	$21\frac{5}{8}$ in. beween tenons
2	Top battens	Walnut	$3/4$	$2\frac{1}{4}$	$12\frac{3}{4}$	
1	Front	Walnut	$9/16$	10	26	
1	Back	Walnut	$9/16$	$12\frac{3}{4}$	26	
2	Ends	Walnut	$9/16$	$12\frac{3}{4}$	$12\frac{5}{8}$	
1	Bottom	Yellow pine	$9/16$	$11\frac{7}{8}$	$25\frac{1}{4}$	
2	Base frames	Yellow pine	$3/4$	2	$24\frac{1}{2}$	22 in. between tenons
2	Base frames	Yellow pine	$3/4$	2	$12\frac{5}{8}$	
1	Base frame	Yellow pine	$3/4$	$2\frac{1}{2}$	$10\frac{5}{8}$	$8\frac{5}{8}$ in. between tenons
1	Drawer guide	Yellow pine	$5/8$	$1\frac{1}{2}$	11	
1	Drawer stile	Walnut	$9/16$	$1\frac{1}{2}$	$3\frac{7}{8}$	
4	Feet	Walnut	$1\frac{1}{16}$	$4\frac{3}{4}$	$8\frac{1}{2}$	Cut to pattern. This makes eight.
1	Corner block	Pine	$7/8$	$7/8$	8	Saw on diagonal. This makes eight.
1	Glue block	Pine	$3/4$	$3/4$	30	This makes eight.
2	Top moldings	Walnut	$5/8$	$7/8$	$27\frac{7}{8}$	Miter, glue, and nail to top.
2	Top moldings	Walnut	$5/8$	$7/8$	14	Miter, glue, and nail to top.
2	Waist moldings	Walnut	$5/16$	$5/8$	$26\frac{5}{8}$	Miter, glue, and nail to chest.
2	Waist moldings	Walnut	$5/16$	$5/8$	$13\frac{1}{4}$	Miter, glue, and nail to chest.
2	Base moldings	Walnut	$3/8$	$3/4$	$26\frac{3}{4}$	Miter, glue, and nail to chest.
2	Base moldings	Walnut	$3/8$	$3/4$	$13\frac{3}{8}$	Miter, glue, and nail to chest.
2	Tray sides	Pine	$1/4$	$2\frac{7}{8}$	$11\frac{1}{2}$	
2	Tray ends	Pine	$1/4$	$2\frac{7}{8}$	$2\frac{1}{2}$	
1	Tray bottom	Pine	$1/4$	3	$11\frac{1}{2}$	
2	Drawer fronts	Walnut	$5/8$	$2\frac{15}{16}$	12	
4	Drawer sides	Pine	$3/8$	$2\frac{11}{16}$	$11\frac{13}{16}$	
2	Drawer backs	Pine	$3/8$	$2\frac{3}{16}$	$11\frac{5}{8}$	
2	Drawer bottoms	Pine	$5/16$	$11\frac{5}{8}$	$11\frac{1}{4}$	

Hardware: 1 chest lock, $3/4$ selvedge to key pin; 2 drawer or till locks, $5/8$ selvedge to key pin; 4 cast brass knobs, $5/8$-in diameter; 1 pr. narrow butt hinges, $1\frac{1}{2}$ in. long bottom is used, disregard this precaution and make the cuts no deeper than the required 3/16 in.

3. The construction shown to secure the battens to the top are the author's, based on similar applications.

4. Mitered feet indicate no spline but blind splines were frequently employed.

5. The ogee feet present no difficult problem. After the eight blocks have been cut out to shape as shown in the sketch, lay off their profile with a pattern placed across the squared end, as indicated by the dotted line. The blocks may now be fastened, one at a time, to a vertical sawing block and band-sawed to shape. Lacking a band saw, the job may be done right on the workbench with plane and gouge. Miter after shaping, glue together in pairs (splining is recommended), and then do the final smoothing and sanding to shape after the glue has set.

Block of wood for ogee feet

6. The tray is not a sliding or removable one and so may be made of only two pieces, one side and a bottom. If the tray is to be made of two pieces, change the bill, making each piece 3/8 in. longer and the bottom 3/16 in. wider than shown. Dado each end 3/16 in. deep into the chest front and back, and groove the bottom 3/16 in. into the chest end.

WINDSOR CHAIR

This is one of the simplest chairs of the Windsor type to be found. It is a degraded one when purity of style is thought of. Fairly common in the Virginia mountains, others closely akin to it have been seen by the writer in Kentucky and North Carolina.

It is a real job to build the ordinary Windsor chair in the amateur craftsman's shop, but this simple one presents no problem that the average woodworker cannot solve.

CONSTRUCTION NOTES

1. Turn all legs, stretchers, and spindles, and sand them ready for assembly, but leave the lathe-centered ends on them. See construction note No. 6 below. Spindles and stretchers may be turned without shoulders, if desired, and the spindles may be worked out with a spokeshave by hand instead of by turning. Many old ones were so made. Spindles, stretchers, and back posts should be thoroughly dry. Seats, legs, and top rails that were somewhat green were used purposely. In his book, *A Windsor Handbook*, Wallace Nutting, writing about Windsor chair construction, wrote:

"The spindles, of course, were dry. This made them rigid when green seat and bow shrunk around them; and a well-made chair was like one solid, airy shape of wood, so well done that many are without a loose joint today, after the use and abuse of four or five generations."

2. Saw out the seat but do not scoop it out or shape its edges until after all holes have been bored.

3. Spot the centers of the spindle and leg holes and bore, using the bit sizes indicated. If a bit brace is used, clamp the seat firmly to a worktable top. Using two bevel squares, one set for the angle to hold the bit forward or back, the other to hold the bit over to the left or right, bore holes to the depth indicated. If a perfect job is not done, take comfort in the fact that neither did the mountain craftsman of long ago who made the original do a perfect job; but the chances are that you will be surprised and pleased at how well you will do.

4. Leg and back-post holes may be tapered with the correct size of repairman's reamer. Such reamer dimensions may be different from the ones shown, and so, turn the tenon ends to correspond to the taper used. If preferred, bore straight holes and turn corresponding straight tenons on legs and posts, leaving a slight shoulder on each.

5. Shape the seat edges as indicated.

6. Make a boring jig with centers to hold the legs and stretchers while they are bored, so that the angles will correspond to those shown. Such a device is shown in the sketch. It will be found useful whether boring the holes on a drill press or by hand with a bit brace.

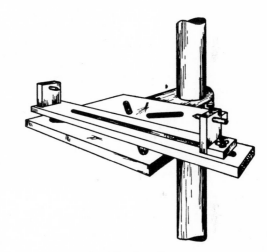

Boring jig

Bill of Materials

PIECES	ARTICLE	KIND OF WOOD	THICKNESS	WIDTH	LENGTH	REMARKS
1	Seat	White pine or poplar	1¾	16	15¹³⁄₁₆	
2	Front legs	Hickory	1½	1½	18¼	½ in. for lathe centers
2	Back legs	Hickory	1½	1½	17¼	½ in. for lathe centers
2	Side stretchers	Hickory	1½	1½	14¾	½ in. for lathe centers
1	Center stretcher	Hickory	1⅛	1⅛	15¾	½ in. for lathe centers
1	Top rail	Poplar	2⅜	3	20½	Taper saw to shape.
2	Back posts	Hickory	1⅛	1⅛	18½	½ in. for lathe centers
5	Back spindles	Hickory	¾	¾	16¾	Extra for lathe centers

NOTE: Maple may be used for legs, stretchers, and back posts. It is white and hard and used in most Windsors, but it is not as tough as hickory.

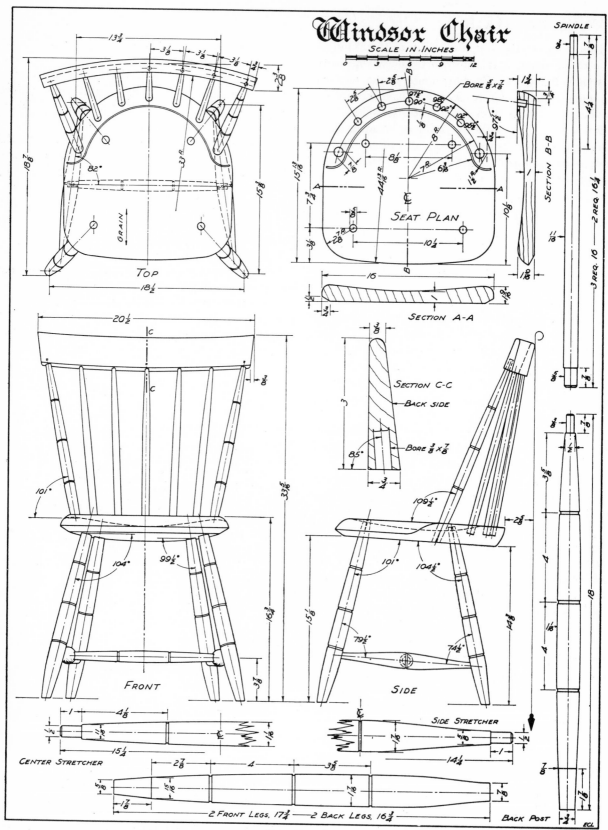

Windsor Chair

SCALE IN INCHES

Seat Plan

Section A-A

Section B-B

Section C-C
BACK SIDE
Bore $\frac{3}{8}$ X $\frac{7}{8}$

Top

Front

Side

SPINDLE

Center Stretcher

Side Stretcher

Back Post

2 Front Legs, 17$\frac{3}{4}$ — 2 Back Legs, 16$\frac{3}{4}$

PLATE 15

48

7. Dry assemble the chair from the seat down. When it is seen that the legs fit, remove them by pairs with their respective side stretchers. Now glue up these legs and stretchers, twisting them into the position they will occupy when in the seat of the chair. Pin stretcher tenons with ⅛ by ⅛ by 1-in. hickory pins driven into ⅛-in. diameter holes drilled through the sides of the legs and through the tenons. Allow this to dry.

8. Glue the center stretcher into the side stretchers and the legs into the seat in the same operation, having previously made thin saw kerfs 1¼ in. deep across the diameters of the legs at 90 deg. to the grain of the seat. Dip long thin hickory wedges into glue, insert them into kerfs, and drive them in hard. Allow all of this to dry.

9. The seat now is ready to be scooped out for added comfort. Use a wide shallow-sweep gouge. Old-timers used foot or hand adzes for this work. Use a ⅛-in. veining tool to carve the decoration line around the seat in front of the back spindles. A flexible shaft sander will be found useful to sand the seat after it has been scooped out. The job is not hard by hand, however, using a block and coarse garnet paper.

10. Now for the back. Put both back posts and the center spindle in place. By sighting a little you will see how to bore the holes that have already been spotted on the underedge of the top rail. Bore, say, the center spindle hole; place the rail on that spindle, and check positions and angles of other holes.

Queen Anne Side Chair

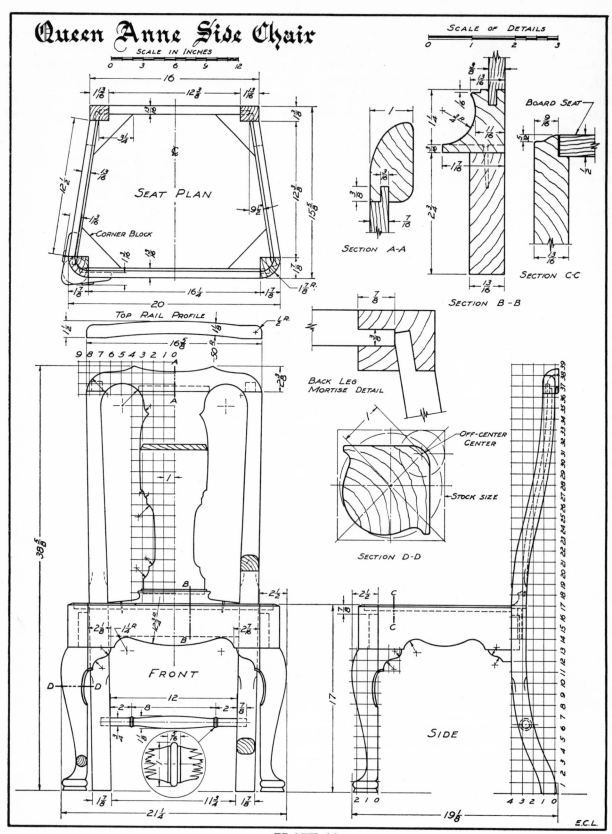

SCALE OF DETAILS

SCALE IN INCHES

SEAT PLAN

CORNER BLOCK

TOP RAIL PROFILE

SECTION A-A

SECTION B-B

SECTION C-C

BOARD SEAT

BACK LEG
MORTISE DETAIL

OFF-CENTER
CENTER

STOCK SIZE

SECTION D-D

FRONT

SIDE

E.C.L.

PLATE 16

QUEEN ANNE SIDE CHAIR

This exquisite example of the period known as Queen Anne is at Williamsburg, Virginia. It is not a difficult chair to build and may well be undertaken by many of the readers of this work. It will serve so well as either desk, dining, or occasional chair that it is worth the effort.

You may prefer to make a padded seat, but the original has a solid board slip seat that is more comfortable than one would imagine.

Like all Queen Anne designs, it requires large pieces of valuable lumber. Walnut was cheap and plentiful when this chair was built. Though not nearly as plentiful today, the sizes called for may be purchased in large lumberyards over the country.

CONSTRUCTION NOTES

1. The front legs are worked out of solid blocks 2½ in. square. While square, the blocks are mounted in a lathe on true centers and the raised pad feet are turned. Turning is done at the tailstock end. Then, on the proper diagonal, the foot end of the block is put in the lathe 1 in. off center toward what is to be the ankle of the leg. The top end is set off center 1 in. on the other side of dead center on the same diagonal and the ankle of the leg is turned. The block is next marked with a profile pattern on two adjacent sides and sawed roughly to shape. The rest of the work must be done with spokeshave, chisel, gouge, and file. It is a help to cut the mortises before bandsawing the blocks, because a completely worked Queen Anne leg presents clamping problems.

2. Make the splat pattern just a trifle longer than the drawing indicates to allow for its reverse-curve profile. Saw out the splat to the correct profile and then to the shape shown in the front view. Mortise it into the top rail, but do not shoulder the lower tenon until the chair has been partially dry-assembled, and the cut in the shoulder can be marked.

Bill of Materials

PIECES	ARTICLE	KIND OF WOOD	THICKNESS	WIDTH	LENGTH	REMARKS
2	Front legs	Walnut	2¾	2¾	17	
1	Back leg	Walnut	113/16	6	36⅜	This makes two.
1	Front rail	Walnut	13/16	3 15/16	18 1/16	7/16-in. shoulders, face side; 16¼ in. between tenons
2	Side rails	Walnut	13/16	3 15/16	14¼	7/16-in. shoulder, face side of front end; 12½ in. between tenons.
1	Back rail	Walnut	13/16	2¾	14⅛	12⅜ in. between tenons
1	Back stretcher	Walnut	1⅛	1⅛	14	No shoulders on ends
1	Top rail	Walnut	1½	2⅜	16 9/16	Cut to pattern.
1	Splat	Walnut	13/16	6⅝	19½	18 in. between tenons
1	Splat bottom rail	Walnut	1 7/16	1 7/16	12½	
4	Leg blocks	Walnut	1½	2¼	2¼	Cut to fit leg.
2	Back-leg blocks	Walnut	13/16	1	2⅛	
1	Seat	Walnut	½	13½	18⅞	Cut to fit recess. ⅛-in. clearance has been allowed from front to back.
	For those who prefer a padded seat:					
1	Front-seat frame	Oak	¾	1½	18⅞	Through-mortise joints
1	Back-seat frame	Oak	¾	1½	14¾	Through-mortise joints
2	Side-seat frames	Oak	¾	1½	13½	Through-mortise joints

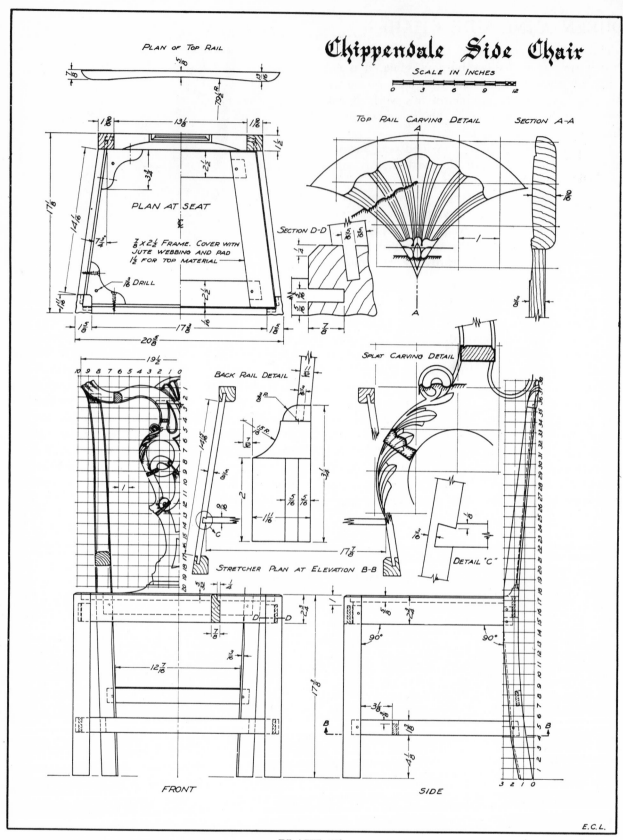

PLAN OF TOP RAIL

Chippendale Side Chair

SCALE IN INCHES

0   3   6   9   12

PLAN AT SEAT

⅞ x 2½ FRAME. COVER WITH
JUTE WEBBING AND PAD
1½ FOR TOP MATERIAL

TOP RAIL CARVING DETAIL

SECTION A-A

SECTION D-D

⅛ DRILL

BACK RAIL DETAIL

SPLAT CARVING DETAIL

DETAIL "C"

STRETCHER PLAN AT ELEVATION B-B

FRONT

SIDE

E.C.L.

PLATE 17

CHIPPENDALE SIDE CHAIR (Ribbon Back)

Another and different example of magnificent Chippendale has come down to us in this intertwined ribbon-back chair. It is made of dense blood-red mahogany and is strong, heavy, and in a state of almost perfect preservation.

CONSTRUCTION NOTES

1. A study of the drawing will convince the man who would build this chair that, while tedious, the carving may be undertaken with confidence. It is not deep carving; much of it can be done with a flat chisel or a skew chisel; you assuredly will not have wood harder to carve than the original builder; and, furthermore, he was a mere man perhaps no more gifted than you.

2. Build up the back, leaving a tab or ear on each end of the top rail to be used in clamping it to the

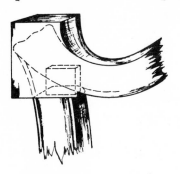

Tab on end of top rail

back legs. After the glue has dried, saw off the tabs and finish carving the top rail.

3. Do not cut tenons on the splat until you check the distance from the back-rail mortise to the top-rail mortise.

4. Back-leg beading can be put on with a scratch stock. A scratch stock can be made to give the front legs their very shallow molded sides. In fact, a scratch stock with a blade made from a piece of high-speed steel machine hack-saw blade is an efficient tool.

Bill of Materials

PIECES	ARTICLE	KIND OF WOOD	THICKNESS	WIDTH	LENGTH	REMARKS
1	Back leg	Mahogany	1⁹⁄₁₆	4¾	36½	This makes two.
2	Front legs	Mahogany	1⅝	1¹¹⁄₁₆	17⅜	
1	Top rail	Mahogany	⅞	2¾	20	See construction note 2.
1	Splat	Mahogany	⅜	8	17½	16¹³⁄₁₆ in. between tenons
1	Front rail	Mahogany	⅞	2¾	19⅛	17⅜ in. between tenons
2	Side rails	Mahogany	⅞	2¾	15¹³⁄₁₆	14¹⁄₁₆ in. between tenons
1	Back rail	Mahogany	1¹¹⁄₁₆	3¼	14⅞	13⅛ in. between tenons, long point
2	Side stretchers	Mahogany	⅝	1⅜	16¹¹⁄₁₆	14¹⁵⁄₁₆ in. between tenons, long point
1	Center stretcher	Mahogany	⁹⁄₁₆	1⅜	18¾	17⅞ in. between tenons, long point
1	Back stretcher	Mahogany	⅝	1⅜	14³⁄₁₆	12⁷⁄₁₆ in. between tenons, long point
1	Front-seat frame	Oak	⅞	2½	15½	14 in. between tenons, long point
1	Back-seat frame	Oak	⅞	2½	13	10½ in. between tenons, long point
2	Side-seat frames	Oak	⅞	2½	15¼	
4	Corner blocks	Oak	1½	3¾	4	

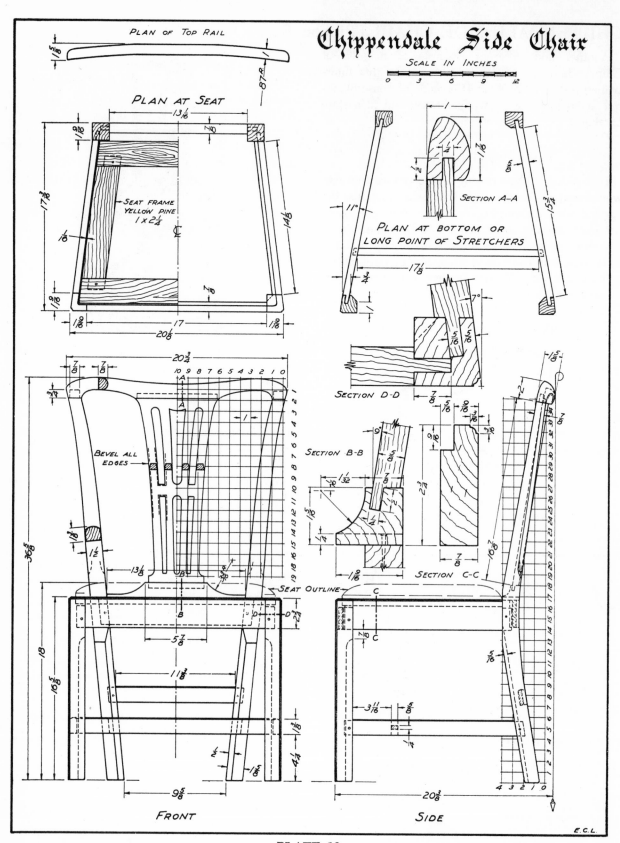

PLAN OF TOP RAIL

Chippendale Side Chair

SCALE IN INCHES

PLAN AT SEAT

SEAT FRAME
YELLOW PINE
1 x 2¼

SECTION A-A

PLAN AT BOTTOM OR
LONG POINT OF STRETCHERS

SECTION D-D

SECTION B-B

SECTION C-C

BEVEL ALL
EDGES

SEAT OUTLINE

FRONT

SIDE

PLATE 18

CHIPPENDALE SIDE CHAIR

Restored Williamsburg, Virginia, is visited by large numbers of people, throughout the year, to see the handsome buildings and fine collections of furnishings on display. This Chippendale side chair is one of many originals there. It is representative of Chippendale's later work. As time went on, Thomas Chippendale used more straight lines and less carving. He was quick to adapt new ideas and to change his designs to suit changing tastes. When this chair was made, the style known as Queen Anne, with its many curves, and the exquisitely wrought carvings of Chippendale's earlier work, were losing favor. Here is an example of the plain lines, simple decoration, and increased strength of construction that followed. It is a design not difficult to reproduce in the small shop.

CONSTRUCTION NOTES

1. Notice that the mortises are cut on the angle or flare of the side rails and stretchers. It makes a stronger joint than to cut them at right angles.

2. Study of the drawing will reveal that the face side of the side rails will be a warped surface when made flush to the side of the back legs. This is simple to do. After mortises and tenons have been cut, dry assemble, mark down the shoulder of the back tenon to determine what must come off to make the two surfaces come flush, and then plane that amount off, fairing it back far enough not to be seen. Side stretchers will need like treatment.

3. The plan of the top rail shows that it has a straight section in the center as long as the top of the splat is wide. The ends are curved on an inside radius of 87 deg. The cross section of this rail is shaped like a capital D in the curved portion, the leg of the D being slanted back, to line up with the angle of the back legs; a different cross section prevails along the straight part as at A-A.

Face side of side rails a warped surface

Bill of Materials

PIECES	ARTICLE	KIND OF WOOD	THICKNESS	WIDTH	LENGTH	REMARKS
2	Front legs	Mahogany	$1\frac{9}{16}$	$1\frac{9}{16}$	$16\frac{5}{8}$	
1	Back leg	Mahogany	$1\frac{5}{8}$	$5\frac{1}{2}$	$35\frac{7}{8}$	This makes two.
1	Front rail	Mahogany	$\frac{7}{8}$	$2\frac{3}{4}$	$18\frac{3}{4}$	17 in. between tenons
2	Side rails	Mahogany	$\frac{7}{8}$	$2\frac{3}{4}$	$15\frac{7}{8}$	$14\frac{1}{8}$ in. between tenons; $13\frac{1}{16}$ in. between tenons, long point
1	Back rail	Mahogany	$\frac{7}{8}$	$2\frac{1}{2}$	$14\frac{13}{16}$	
1	Top rail	Mahogany	$1\frac{7}{8}$	2	$20\frac{3}{4}$	$16\frac{7}{8}$ in. between tenons
1	Splat	Mahogany	$\frac{5}{8}$	8	$17\frac{7}{8}$	
1	Splat rail	Mahogany	$1\frac{5}{16}$	$1\frac{9}{16}$	$13\frac{1}{8}$	Work molding and cut to pattern.
2	Side stretchers	Mahogany	$\frac{5}{8}$	$1\frac{3}{8}$	$17\frac{1}{2}$	$15\frac{3}{4}$ in. between tenons, long point
1	Center stretcher	Mahogany	$\frac{5}{8}$	$1\frac{3}{8}$	$18\frac{1}{8}$	$17\frac{1}{8}$ in. between tenons, long point
1	Back stretcher	Mahogany	$\frac{5}{8}$	$1\frac{3}{8}$	$13\frac{1}{8}$	$11\frac{3}{8}$ in. between tenons, long point
1	Seat frame, front	Yellow pine	1	$2\frac{1}{4}$	$18\frac{5}{8}$	
1	Seat frame, back	Yellow pine	1	$2\frac{1}{4}$	$14\frac{7}{8}$	
2	Seat frame, sides	Yellow pine	1	$2\frac{1}{4}$	$12\frac{1}{4}$	$10\frac{1}{4}$ in. between tenons

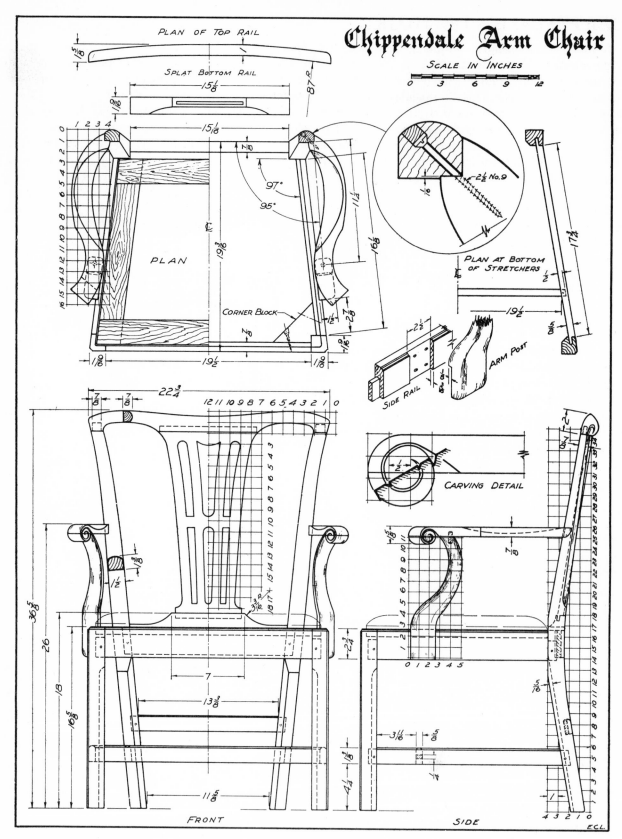

PLATE 19

CHIPPENDALE ARMCHAIR

This armchair is not an original but was designed by the writer to accompany the side chair shown on the preceding pages. It is included in this collection, so that a set of dining chairs may be built. It is 2 in. wider at the back and 2 in. deeper than the side chair, but the angles and bevels are the same.

CONSTRUCTION NOTES

1. Gain out the side rails to take the arm post. Clamp the gained post into the side-rail gain. Place the arm on the post in the position it will occupy, and mark the back leg to be notched out on the front face only. After the notch has been cut, set the arm in place, having inserted a dowel center in the previously drilled hole in the arm post, and mark it to drill. The arm post and arm are now ready to be glued and screwed in place.

2. The seat frame is covered with jute webbing stretched tight as a platform for padding the seat.

Bill of Materials

PIECES	ARTICLE	KIND OF WOOD	THICKNESS	WIDTH	LENGTH	REMARKS
2	Front legs	Mahogany	1 9/16	1 9/16	16 5/8	
1	Back leg	Mahogany	1 5/8	5 1/2	35 7/8	This makes two.
1	Front rail	Mahogany	7/8	2 3/4	21 1/4	19 1/2 in. between tenons
2	Side rails	Mahogany	7/8	2 3/4	17 7/8	16 1/8 in. between tenons
1	Back rail	Mahogany	7/8	2 1/2	16 13/16	15 1/16 in. between tenons, long point
1	Top rail	Mahogany	1 5/8	2	22 3/4	16 7/8 in. between tenons
1	Splat	Mahogany	5/8	10	17 7/8	
1	Splat rail	Mahogany	1 5/16	1 9/16	15 1/8	Work molding and cut to pattern.
2	Side stretchers	Mahogany	5/8	1 3/8	19 1/2	17 3/4 in. between tenons, outside long points
1	Center stretcher	Mahogany	5/8	1 3/8	20 1/2	19 1/2 in. between tenons, long point
1	Back stretcher	Mahogany	5/8	1 3/8	15 1/8	13 3/8 in. between tenons, long point
2	Arms	Mahogany	7/8	3 3/8	16	
2	Arm blocks	Mahogany	7/8	2 3/4	1 3/4	Glue to arms, cut to pattern, carve.
2	Arm posts	Mahogany	1 1/2	5	11 1/4	
1	Seat frame, front	Yellow pine	1	2 1/4	21 1/2	
1	Seat frame, back	Yellow pine	1	2 1/4	17 3/4	
2	Seat frame, sides	Yellow pine	1	2 1/4	17 3/4	

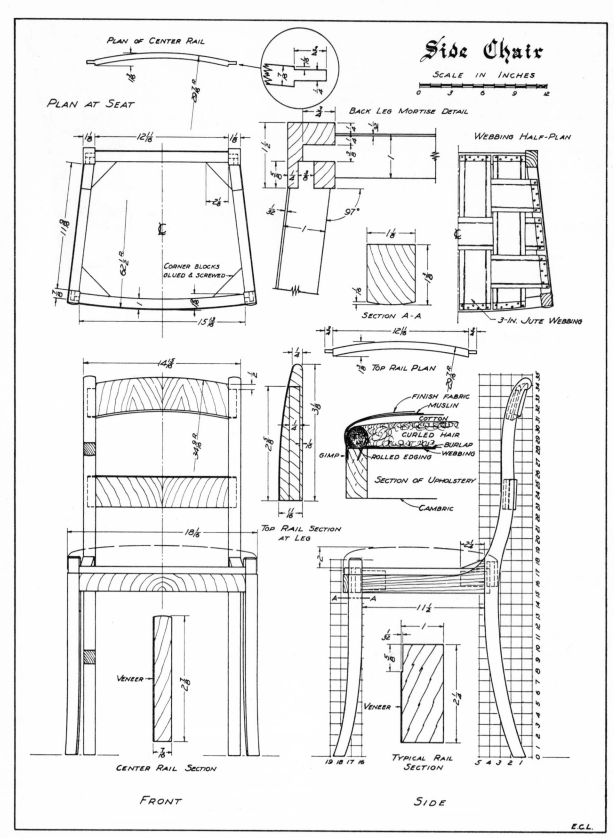

Plan of Center Rail

Plan at Seat

Back Leg Mortise Detail

Side Chair

SCALE IN INCHES

0   3   6   9   12

Corner blocks glued & screwed

Webbing Half-Plan

97°

Section A-A

3-In. Jute Webbing

Top Rail Plan

Finish Fabric
Muslin
Cotton
Curled Hair
Burlap
Gimp
Rolled Edging
Webbing
Section of Upholstery
Cambric

Top Rail Section at Leg

Veneer

Center Rail Section

Front

A ——— A

Veneer

Typical Rail Section

Side

E.C.L.

PLATE 20

SIDE CHAIR

This delicate little side chair was purchased in New Orleans where it was said to have come from England. It is one of a set of four. Woodworms in two of the chestnut rails necessitated major repairs undertaken by an expert cabinetmaker. While in his shop and all to pieces, it was copied. Although its tenons are quite short, splendid fits had been obtained that still held firm.

CONSTRUCTION NOTES

1. Clamp the top-rail veneer onto the rail with sandbags. Veneer is more pliable when kept in a cool damp cellar until just before using, or steamed slightly before working. It must be limber to conform to the double-curved surface of this rail. Match and tape the veneer before gluing.

2. Note that all tenons are cut and mortises made at right angles to the respective surfaces.

3. The chair can be made, of course, without veneer, but Empire pieces count heavily on veneer for decoration.

4. Upholstery is made simpler by reason of no springs, the cushioning effect being secured from the springiness of the curled-hair stuffing.

Bill of Materials

PIECES	ARTICLE	KIND OF WOOD	THICKNESS	WIDTH	LENGTH	REMARKS
1	Back leg	Mahogany	1⅛	6½	35	This makes two.
1	Front leg	Mahogany	1⅛	4¼	18¼	This makes two.
1	Top rail	Mahogany	1⅜	4	14³⁄₁₆	12¹¹⁄₁₆ in. between tenons, centered-matched veneer
1	Center rail	Mahogany	1³⁄₁₆	3	14³⁄₁₆	12¹¹⁄₁₆ in. between tenons, centered-matched veneer
1	Front rail	Chestnut	1½	2¼	17¹⁄₁₆	15¹³⁄₁₆ in. between tenons, long point, centered-matched veneer
2	Side rails	Chestnut	1	2¼	13¹⁄₁₆	11⁹⁄₁₆ in. between tenons, short point, straight veneer
1	Side-rail block	Chestnut	1	1	2¼	This makes two. Glue to, and veneer with, side rails.
1	Back rail	Chestnut	1	2¼	14³⁄₁₆	12¹¹⁄₁₆ in. between tenons, straight-grained veneer
4	Corner blocks	Chestnut	1¾	2¾	3	Fit to frame.
	Veneer as needed					

59

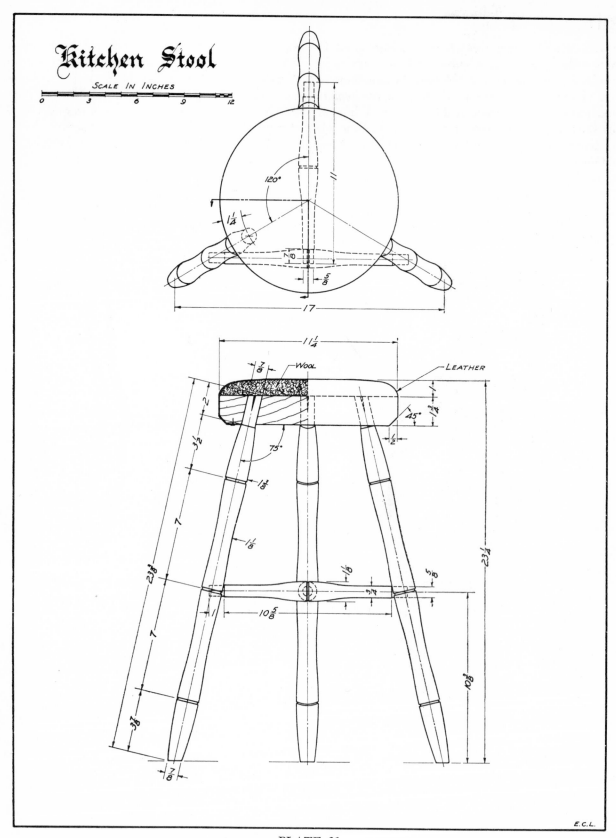

Kitchen Stool

SCALE IN INCHES

PLATE 21

KITCHEN STOOL

Quaintness is not this stool's sole asset, if comfort and utility count for anything in a kitchen. The stool was discovered in the kitchen of a mountain cottage where it looks to have been for at least a hundred years. The thick native white-pine seat is padded with sheep's wool (skin, wool, and all are tacked onto the seat) and that is covered by brown leather. The turnings suggest the later Windsor-chair bamboo turnings.

CONSTRUCTION NOTES

1. Bore leg holes from the underside of the seat.
2. Set the completed stool on a flat surface and mark around each leg with a pencil resting on a ¼-in. block. Saw to the lines made, and the legs will bear flat on the floor.

3. The seat may be padded with fleece or with curled hair for a soft seat, or with Spanish moss covered with a layer of hair for a firm seat. Either glue or tack down the first layer of padding to prevent creeping. A layer of upholstery cotton under the final covering makes a smooth job.

4. Thoroughly dampen the flesh side of the leather before applying. Stretch and work it out to a smooth seat, molding it, as it were, over the edges and around the seat. Allow it to dry for several days before using.

Bill of Materials

PIECES	ARTICLE	KIND OF WOOD	THICKNESS	WIDTH	LENGTH	REMARKS
1	Top	White pine	1¾	11¼	11¼	Saw to shape and chamfer lower edge.
3	Legs	Hickory	1½	1½	24	⅝ in. for spur center
1	Side stretcher	Hickory	1³⁄₁₆	1³⁄₁₆	13¼	⅝ in. for centers
1	Center stretcher	Hickory	1³⁄₁₆	1³⁄₁₆	11⅝	⅝ in. for centers

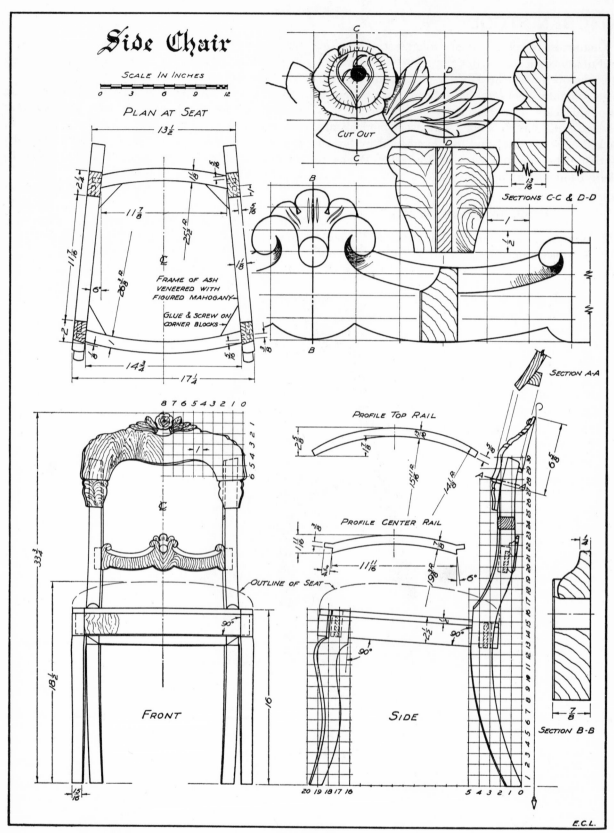

Side Chair

SCALE IN INCHES

0   3   6   9   12

PLAN AT SEAT

13½

FRAME OF ASH
VENEERED WITH
FIGURED MAHOGANY

GLUE & SCREW ON
CORNER BLOCKS

CUT OUT

SECTIONS C-C & D-D

SECTION A-A

PROFILE TOP RAIL

PROFILE CENTER RAIL

OUTLINE OF SEAT

FRONT

SIDE

SECTION B-B

E.C.L.

PLATE 22

SIDE CHAIR (American Empire)

This pretty little American Empire side chair is built of that heavy old mahogany no longer on the market, but a fine reproduction can be made from Peruvian mahogany which is quite hard and not too expensive. The finish on the original is clear shellac that gives to the grain of the wood a clear deep beauty. This chair may have been covered in haircloth and buttoned, but it is now covered with velvet, trimmed with gimp.

CONSTRUCTION NOTES

1. Two or more chairs are cheaper to build than one because of the large pieces required to saw out various members. If the curved rails are sawed from sufficiently wide stock, the outside scraps can be used for gluing forms when the veneer is applied.

2. Smooth up the curved rails' face sides and veneer them. Trim the edges of the pieces of matching veneer to get a good joint, butt them together, and tape one side with gummed paper tape. After glue has been applied to the rail and the veneer, tack the veneer in place with tiny nails to prevent creeping when the clamps are tightened. Be sure that the match line of the veneer is in the center of the rail, and drive the tiny nails where a tenon will be cut, so that, when they are taken out, the piece will not be marred.

Bill of Materials

PIECES	ARTICLE	KIND OF WOOD	THICKNESS	WIDTH	LENGTH	REMARKS
2	Back legs	Mahogany	1⅛	5	30	Cut to pattern.
2	Front legs	Mahogany	1⅛	4	16	Cut to pattern.
2	Side rails	Ash	1⅛	2½	13⁷⁄₁₆	11⁷⁄₁₆ in. between tenons, veneered
1	Front rail	Ash	1⅞	2½	16½	14¾ in. between tenons across long points, cut on radii, veneer.
1	Back rail	Ash	1⅞	2¼	13⅞	11⅞ in. between tenons, long points, cut on radii, and veneer.
1	Center rail	Mahogany	1¹¹⁄₁₆	3½	13³⁄₁₆	11¹¹⁄₁₆ in. between tenons, long points, cut on radii, cut to pattern, crotch veneer, and carve.
1	Top rail	Mahogany	2⅝	6⅝	17	Cut on radii, cut to pattern, crotch veneer, and carve.
2	Top-rail shields	Mahogany	⅜	2⅜	2½	Cut to pattern, crotch veneer.
4	Corner blocks	Chestnut	2	1½	3¼	Cut to a tight fit, glue, and screw into corners after chair is in last clamps.

Crotch veneer as needed.

3. Cut the tenons after the rails have been veneered, as no allowance has been made on the bill for the thickness of the veneer, and the side rails must come flush with the legs.

4. After band-sawing the legs in a production shop, the square edge would be straight-cut and the molded edges would be molded with an elaborate form and a double spindle shaper. That complicated process is not needed in the home or school shop. The chair legs were originally shaped entirely by hand with a spokeshave, file, and scraper. They are perfect but no more so than they can be made with hand tools and a little patience.

5. Cut a $\frac{1}{16}$ by $\frac{1}{2}$-in. rabbet all around this chair except on the back legs to make room for upholstery fabric. Make this $\frac{1}{8}$ in. deep, if needle point is to be the covering.

6. Make accurate well-fitted joints throughout, because the strength of the chair depends on the work done at this point. After cutting all mortises and tenons, dry-assemble the chair and clamp it up as a check. Glue up the sides, pinning joints with $\frac{3}{16}$-in. pins from the inside. When the sides have dried they may be put together with the front and back rails, but these are not pinned. Snug-fitting corner blocks, glued and screwed into the four corners, lend great strength to the chair.

7. Chisel and file away just enough of each back leg to form a bearing for the top rail and two shields under it. The top rail is glued and screwed to the legs from the back, one screw each side with the screwhead under the surface and a flat-grained wood plug used to hide it. Glue alone holds the shields.

8. Upholster the frame as you would any similar piece. The original has four springs resting on the webbing.

CHEST OF DRAWERS

A splendid example of Southern workmanship is to be seen in this chest of drawers of wild cherry copied in Staunton, Virginia. Its quarter columns, ogee bracket feet, beaded drawer fronts, and its proportions bespeak the influence of the great Thomas Chippendale. It is a dark, rich, reddish-brown color that might be mistaken for mahogany, although no stain was ever used on it.

It is a true chest, inasmuch as both top and bot-tom are solid and dovetailed into the sides. Bottom, back, and drawers, save the fronts, are Southern yellow pine, and the drawer bottoms are single boards. The feet are fastened to the chest bottom with corner blocks glued and nailed in place.

A rare feature is the overhanging top at the back. This was obviously designed to fit against the wall, bridging the gap between chest and wall caused by the baseboard.

Bill of Materials

PIECES	ARTICLE	KIND OF WOOD	THICKNESS	WIDTH	LENGTH	REMARKS
1	Top	Cherry	7/8	21	39 1/8	
2	Sides	Cherry	7/8	17 15/16	28 1/4	3/4-in. dovetail pins, top end; 7/8-in. pins, bottom
1	Bottom	Yellow pine	7/8	18 5/8	38 7/8	37 3/8 in. between dovetails
1	Bottom facing	Cherry	1/4	7/8	35 1/2	
1	Top rail	Cherry	1	2 3/4	38 5/8	37 3/8 in. between tenons
3	Drawer rails	Cherry	7/8	2 3/4	38 5/8	37 3/8 in. between dovetails
2	Corner posts	Cherry	7/8	15/16	27 1/2	
2	Quarter columns	Cherry	15/16	15/16	27 1/2	Turn and flute.
1	Top molding	Cherry	5/8	1	40 5/8	Miter and nail to top edge.
2	Top moldings	Cherry	5/8	1	21 5/8	Miter and nail to top edge.
1	Base molding	Cherry	5/8	7/8	40 5/8	Miter and nail to base frame.
2	Base moldings	Cherry	5/8	7/8	19 1/2	Miter and nail to base frame.
1	Base-frame front	Pine	7/8	2 3/4	39 1/8	
2	Base-frame sides	Pine	7/8	2 3/4	16 5/8	1 1/4-in. tenon, one end
1	Back	Pine	3/4	27 3/4	38 3/8	Allow extra width for tongues.
4	Front feet	Cherry	1	4 5/8	7 1/4	Miter and cut to pattern; spline and glue together.
2	Back feet	Cherry	1	4 5/8	6 3/4	Cut to pattern.
2	Back feet	Pine	3/4	5 1/2	8	
	Glue blocks as needed	Pine	7/8	7/8		
6	Drawer runners	Pine	7/8	2	15 1/4	1/2-in. tenon, front end
8	Drawer guides	Pine	3/4	15/16	16 1/2	3/8 by 1/4 tongue fits into dado in chest sides.
2	Drawer runners	Pine	7/8	1 3/4	14 3/4	
	Drawers					
1	Front	Cherry	7/8	3 15/16	35 7/16	Rabbet drawer ends to take 1/8 by 5/16 astragal.
1	Front	Cherry	7/8	4 15/16	35 7/16	
1	Front	Cherry	7/8	5 15/16	35 7/16	
1	Front	Cherry	7/8	6 15/16	35 7/16	
2	Sides	Pine	5/8	4 1/8	17	
2	Sides	Pine	5/8	5 1/8	17	
2	Sides	Pine	5/8	6 1/8	17	
2	Sides	Pine	5/8	7 1/8	17	
1	Back	Pine	5/8	3 1/4	35 7/16	
1	Back	Pine	5/8	4 1/4	35 7/16	
1	Back	Pine	5/8	5 1/4	35 7/16	
1	Back	Pine	5/8	6 1/4	35 7/16	
4	Bottoms	Pine	1/2	16 3/4	34 15/16	Groove 1/4 by 3/8 into front and sides.
8	Bead moldings	Cherry	1/8	15/16	35 7/16	Miter 5/16 in. for end bead or astragal.
2	Bead moldings	Cherry	1/8	5/16	25	Miter to fit.

Hardware: 8 ring pulls; 4 escutcheons (Ball, No. 422, 1 1/8 by 1 3/4); 4 till locks for drawers

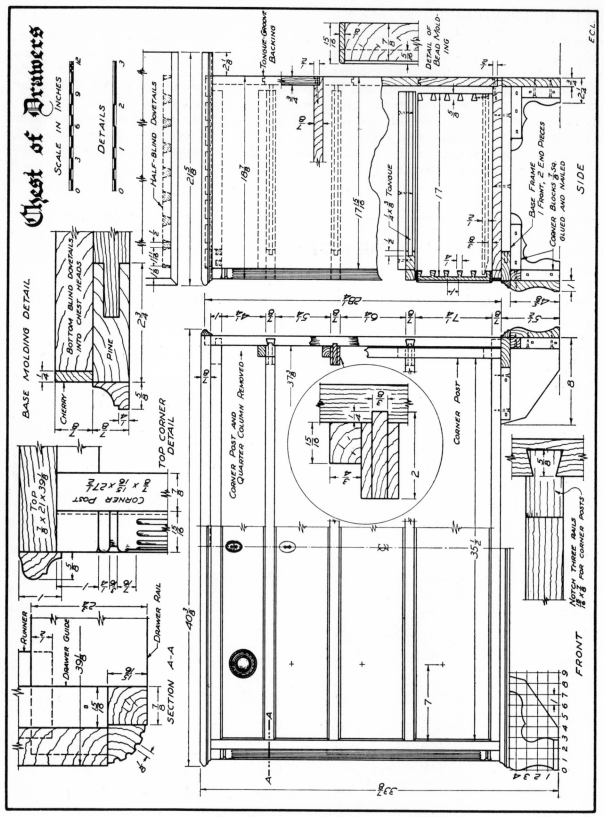

Chest of Drawers

PLATE 23

66

CONSTRUCTION NOTES

1. The top molding covers the half-blind dovetails. Pins cut ¾ in. deep into the underside of the top. These are glued together in the final assembly and may be further strengthened by drilling ³⁄₁₆ by 1½-in. holes through several of the dovetail pins, and driving in ³⁄₁₆ by ³⁄₁₆ by 1½-in. cherry pins.

2. Half-blind dovetails ¾ in. long are visible on the underneath side of the chest bottom.

3. The front top molding should be glued in place. Glue should be applied to the miter joints and about 2 in. along the side. The remaining portion of the end moldings should be nailed and not glued. Tops will spread and contract with changes in humidity and burst if restrained too much. This same note of caution applies to the drawer runners that, on this chest, are dadoed into the sides. Keep these joints dry. A screw or two will hold the runners in place. The runners are nailed into the grooves on the original.

4. The base of the chest, made up of a frame, U-shaped, base molding, and attached feet is a unit that is nailed onto the bottom of the chest proper. Modern use favors screws.

5. A piece of scrap wood ¹⁵⁄₁₆ by 1⅞ by 28⅛ in. should be used to back up the two quarter-column pieces for turning. Glue all three together with paper between the joints; turn; split apart.

6. Use a double-tenon mortise on the top-drawer rail and dovetail the others into the chest heads. Quarter columns will, of course, cover dovetails.

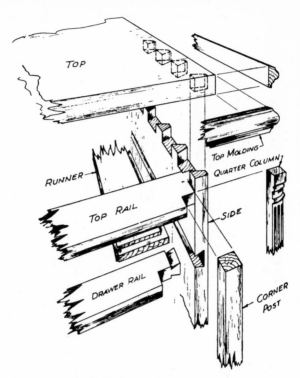

Exploded view of top corner

7. Glue up the ogee feet in pairs with a spline (or the more modern clamp nail) used to further strengthen the joints. Glue blocks are then applied in the corners and along the top edges of each piece. When dry, clean up the top edges and glue and nail or screw them to the underside of the base frame. The base molding has previously been glued tight to the base frame.

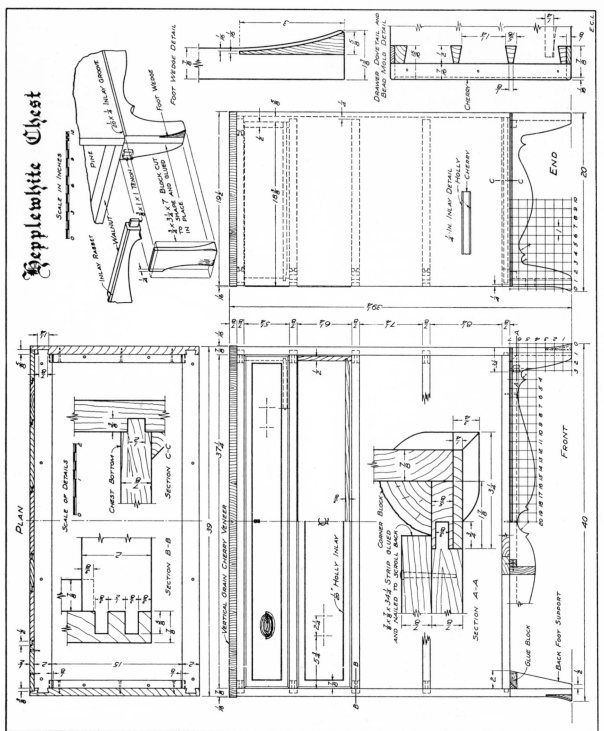

Hepplewhite Chest

PLATE 24

68

HEPPLEWHITE CHEST

This chest was copied in the cabinet shop of Mr. Clinton Varner in Lexington, Virginia. Mr. Varner had learned his trade from his father who, though he had lost his left arm in the War between the States, continued to practice his trade afterward, working with one arm and a stub. His only power tool was a foot-power lathe which he managed to use while holding the chisels and gouges in his only hand, their long handles pressed against his side by his forearm.

Numerous chests of drawers reflecting Mr. Hepplewhite's strong influence are to be found throughout the South. The author has seen six in one home, no two alike. The one depicted here has graceful lines, the traditional French foot, is beautifully proportioned, may serve as either bedroom or dining-room piece, and is one readily reproduced in a small shop. Its black-walnut mass is high-lighted by wild cherry vertical-grain veneer all around the top and by cherry astragals and holly line inlay on the drawers. It is further lightened by a 1/4-in. wide inlay band around its base just below the bottom drawer rail.

Although a close reproduction of the original brass pulls is to be had, many other pulls of this period await the craftman's choice. It may be difficult to obtain drawer locks with a distance of 1 3/8 in. from selvedge to key pin. This will necessitate moving the escutcheon up, perhaps to the center of the inlay line. A suggested departure, still perfectly authentic, is to substitute a diamond-shaped maple-inlaid escutcheon for the brass thread escutcheon found on the original.

Bill of Materials

PIECES	ARTICLE	KIND OF WOOD	THICKNESS	WIDTH	LENGTH	REMARKS
1	Top	Walnut	7/8	19 1/2	39	
2	Sides	Walnut	7/8	19 1/2	38 3/8	
4	Drawer rails	Walnut	7/8	2	38 1/2	37 1/4 in. beween tenons
1	Drawer-back rail	Pine	7/8	2	38 1/2	37 1/4 in. beween tenons
1	Bottom	Pine	7/8	17	38	37 1/4 in. beween tenons
1	Bottom facing	Walnut	7/8	2	38	37 1/4 in. between tenons; glue to front edge of bottom.
1	Apron	Walnut	7/8	3	34	32 1/2 in. between tenons; cut to pattern.
1	Apron strip	Pine	7/8	7/8	34	
2	Front-foot blocks	Pine	5/8	1 7/8	7	Cut to pattern.
2	Front-foot face blocks	Walnut	3/4	3 1/4	7	Cut to pattern.
1	Back-foot support	Pine	7/8	2 5/8	7	This makes two.
2	Foot wedges	Walnut	3/4	2 1/8	3	This makes four.
2	Drawer runners	Pine	7/8	7/8	15 3/4	14 3/4 in. between tenons
6	Drawer runners	Pine	7/8	7/8	17	3/8-in. tenon, one end
	Drawers					
1	Front	Walnut	7/8	4 15/16	37 3/16	1/16-in. vertical clearance has been figured. Another 1/32 in. would not be too much. Left to discretion of builder.
1	Front	Walnut	7/8	5 15/16	37 3/16	1/16-in. vertical clearance has been figured. Another 1/32 in. would not be too much. Left to discretion of builder.
1	Front	Walnut	7/8	6 15/16	37 3/16	
1	Front	Walnut	7/8	7 15/16	37 3/16	
2	Sides	Pine	1/2	5 3/16	18	
2	Sides	Pine	1/2	6 3/16	18	
2	Sides	Pine	1/2	7 3/16	18	
2	Sides	Pine	1/2	8 3/16	18	
1	Back	Pine	1/2	4 7/16	37 3/16	
1	Back	Pine	1/2	5 7/16	37 3/16	
1	Back	Pine	1/2	6 7/16	37 3/16	
1	Back	Pine	1/2	7 7/16	37 3/16	
4	Bottoms	Poplar	3/8	17 3/4	36 11/16	
8	Bead moldings	Cherry	1/8	15/16	38	
8	Bead moldings	Cherry	1/8	7/16	8 1/2	
	Backing	Pine	1/2	38 1/4	31 3/8	Shiplapped 1/2 in.
	Top-edge veneer	Cherry	1/16	80	1	

Hardware: 8 drawer pulls (Ball, No. 3202); 4 drawer locks, till, 1 3/8 in. selvedge to key pin; 2 1/2 yds. 1/20 by 1/4 band inlay; 10 yds. 1/20 by 1/16 holly inlay; 4 brass thread escutcheons

CONSTRUCTION NOTES

1. A number of ways to obtain the slightly curved French foot were used, but this has the advantage of allowing the grain of the chest side to continue to the floor. Make a saw kerf $\frac{1}{16}$ in. from the surface of the sides as shown, 3 in. deep. Sponge the wood to be bent with warm water until you can feel it become flexible. Work glue into the kerf; apply glue to both sides of the wedge, and carefully drive it up into the kerf. Cold-water glue is recommended for this job. Finally, clamp up the feet overnight, using properly shaped clamp blocks.

2. Drawer-front ends must all be rabbeted $\frac{1}{8}$ by $\frac{3}{8}$ in. for the astragal. The bead is laid over the whole width of the top and bottom edges. A combination miter and butt joint is used as shown in the sketch.

3. Drawer sides dovetail into drawer backs with through dovetails. This was almost universal practice among cabinetmakers long ago.

4. Vertical-grain cherry veneer $\frac{1}{16}$ in. thick must be made in the shop, since it is not a ready item on the market.

5. A solid pine bottom rabbeted into the sides and glued is further secured with glue blocks in

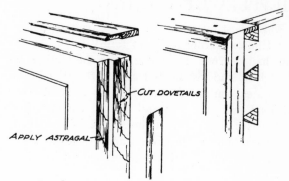

Bead molding applied to drawer front

the original. A $\frac{7}{8}$ by $\frac{7}{8}$ by 16-in. strip screwed up onto the bottom and onto the chest sides (using slotted holes and roundhead screws with washers under the heads) will increase the strength of the piece. A stopped dovetail dado joint would be even better but is more troublesome to make. A third departure from the original construction would replace the solid bottom with a drawer frame mortised together, complete with dust bottom.

6. A favorite way to stop flush drawers was and is to glue and nail thin strips to the top side of the drawer rails where the front will strike them. This old chest was so made.

INLAID CHEST OF DRAWERS

In much of the furniture made in the South there was a blending of periods. Cabinetmakers did not hesitate to combine Chippendale with Hepplewhite to secure an effect that satisfied them or their customers, and this inlaid chest of drawers is an example. Line and mass after Chippendale, inlay imitative of Hepplewhite with a distinct touch of the German and Swiss influence are typical of work produced in the Shenandoah Valley of Virginia. Its rich brown walnut, white holly inlay, and gleaming brass pulls give this piece a rich appearance.

CONSTRUCTION NOTES

1. This is a true chest like the four-drawer Chippendale chest elsewhere in this collection, built by dovetailing the sides, top, and bottom together.

2. The front feet are mitered and either splined or secret dovetailed, while the back feet are dovetailed with the tails exposed on the back. Corner glue blocks strengthen the feet; others are used to fasten the feet to the chest.

3. Escutcheons must center over the key pins of the locks obtainable. Locks should be the old till type with the key pin 1 in. below the selvedge.

4. The bill of material allows $\frac{1}{16}$-in. vertical play for the drawer fronts, sides, and backs. If more is thought necessary, allow it before working for inlay.

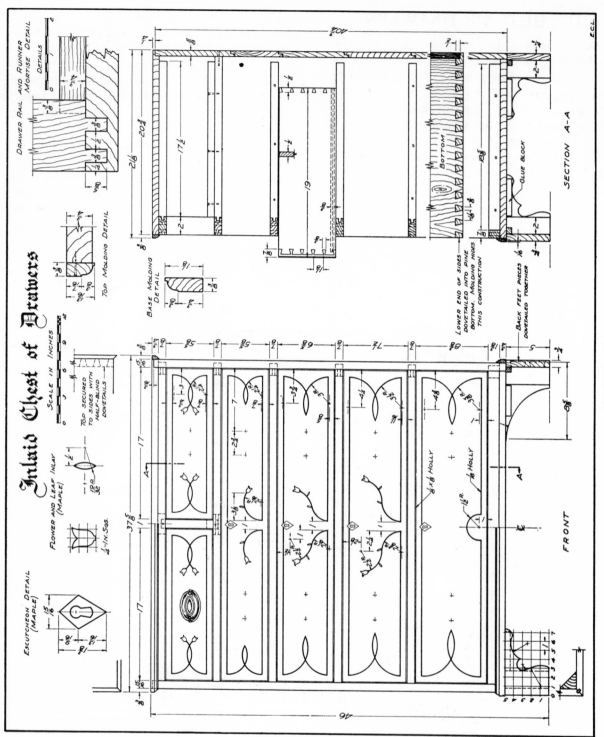

Inlaid Chest of Drawers

PLATE 25

72

Bill of Materials

PIECES	ARTICLE	KIND OF WOOD	THICKNESS	WIDTH	LENGTH	REMARKS
1	Top	Walnut	$\frac{3}{4}$	$20\frac{3}{4}$	$36\frac{7}{8}$	
2	Sides	Walnut	$\frac{15}{16}$	$20\frac{3}{4}$	$40\frac{13}{16}$	
5	Drawer rails	Walnut	$\frac{7}{8}$	2	$36\frac{1}{4}$	35 in. between tenons
1	Drawer rail	Walnut	$\frac{7}{8}$	$1\frac{3}{8}$	$36\frac{1}{4}$	35 in. between tenons
1	Drawer stile	Walnut	1	2	$6\frac{5}{8}$	$5\frac{5}{8}$ in. between tenons
1	Bottom	Yellow pine	$\frac{3}{4}$	$20\frac{1}{8}$	$36\frac{7}{8}$	Shiplapped boards
1	Back	Yellow pine	$\frac{5}{8}$	$40\frac{3}{4}$	36	
1	Top molding	Walnut	$\frac{3}{8}$	$1\frac{3}{16}$	$37\frac{5}{8}$	Miter.
2	Top moldings	Walnut	$\frac{3}{8}$	$1\frac{3}{16}$	$21\frac{1}{8}$	Miter.
1	Base molding	Walnut	$\frac{3}{8}$	$1\frac{1}{8}$	$37\frac{5}{8}$	Miter.
2	Base moldings	Walnut	$\frac{3}{8}$	$1\frac{1}{8}$	$21\frac{1}{8}$	Miter.
6	Feet	Walnut	$\frac{3}{4}$	5	$7\frac{1}{2}$	
2	Back feet	Yellow pine	$\frac{3}{4}$	5	$8\frac{5}{8}$	
2	Glue blocks	Yellow pine	2	2	5	Split diagonally to make four.
8	Glue blocks	Yellow pine	$\frac{3}{4}$	$\frac{3}{4}$	4	
10	Drawer runners	Yellow pine	$\frac{3}{4}$	$\frac{7}{8}$	$17\frac{7}{8}$	$\frac{3}{8}$-in. tenon, one end
2	Drawer runners	Yellow pine	$\frac{3}{4}$	$1\frac{3}{8}$	$18\frac{5}{8}$	
2	Drawer runners	Yellow pine	$\frac{7}{8}$	$2\frac{1}{4}$	$17\frac{7}{8}$	$\frac{3}{8}$-in. tenon, one end
1	Drawer guide	Yellow pine	$\frac{3}{4}$	1	$17\frac{1}{2}$	
	Drawers					
2	Fronts	Walnut	$\frac{7}{8}$	$5\frac{9}{16}$	$16\frac{15}{16}$	
1	Front	Walnut	$\frac{7}{8}$	$5\frac{9}{16}$	$34\frac{15}{16}$	
1	Front	Walnut	$\frac{7}{8}$	$6\frac{9}{16}$	$34\frac{15}{16}$	
1	Front	Walnut	$\frac{7}{8}$	$7\frac{7}{16}$	$34\frac{15}{16}$	
1	Front	Walnut	$\frac{7}{8}$	$8\frac{5}{16}$	$34\frac{15}{16}$	
6	Sides	Yellow pine	$\frac{1}{2}$	$5\frac{9}{16}$	$18\frac{5}{8}$	
2	Sides	Yellow pine	$\frac{1}{2}$	$6\frac{9}{16}$	$18\frac{5}{8}$	
2	Sides	Yellow pine	$\frac{1}{2}$	$7\frac{7}{16}$	$18\frac{5}{8}$	
2	Sides	Yellow pine	$\frac{1}{2}$	$8\frac{5}{16}$	$18\frac{5}{8}$	
2	Backs	Yellow pine	$\frac{1}{2}$	$4\frac{15}{16}$	$16\frac{15}{16}$	
1	Back	Yellow pine	$\frac{1}{2}$	$4\frac{15}{16}$	$34\frac{15}{16}$	
1	Back	Yellow pine	$\frac{1}{2}$	$5\frac{15}{16}$	$34\frac{15}{16}$	
1	Back	Yellow pine	$\frac{1}{2}$	$6\frac{13}{16}$	$34\frac{15}{16}$	
1	Back	Yellow pine	$\frac{1}{2}$	$7\frac{11}{16}$	$34\frac{15}{16}$	
2	Bottoms	Yellow pine	$\frac{3}{8}$	$18\frac{3}{8}$	$16\frac{7}{16}$	Groove $\frac{1}{4}$ in. into front and sides.
4	Bottoms	Yellow pine	$\frac{3}{8}$	$18\frac{3}{8}$	$34\frac{7}{16}$	Groove $\frac{1}{4}$ in. into front and sides.

15 yds. $\frac{1}{8}$ by $\frac{1}{8}$ holly **inlay**
18 yds. $\frac{1}{20}$ by $\frac{1}{16}$ holly inlay
Hardware: 10 pulls (Ball, No. 3217, $2\frac{5}{8}$-in. bore); 4 till locks, 1-in. selvedge to key pin

Queen Anne Highboy

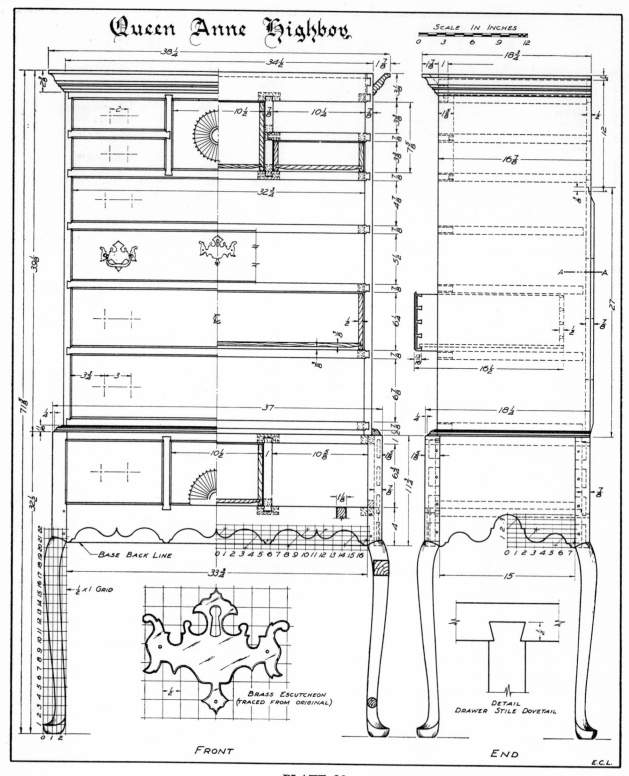

SCALE IN INCHES
0   3   6   9   12

BASE BACK LINE

½ x 1 GRID

BRASS ESCUTCHEON
(TRACED FROM ORIGINAL)

DETAIL
DRAWER STILE DOVETAIL

FRONT

END

E.C.L.

PLATE 26

QUEEN ANNE HIGHBOY

A bride of twenty years ago wanted a chest. Her professor husband mentioned that there was an old one out in the woodshed at his home, but he didn't imagine that she would have the old thing. This cherry highboy is that old chest. No major repairs were necessary, and some of the original hardware was on it. It has unusually graceful legs that, with the scrolled front apron, sunburst carving, and intricate brass pulls, give it an air of delicacy for all its mass. Like all such pieces, it is built in two sections with the top resting on the base.

CONSTRUCTION NOTES

1. Your author has no explanation to offer for the unique joint used to fasten the drawer rails into the chest sides. It is a dovetail joint combined with a dado. The vertical drawer stiles employ the regular dovetailed dado much used by old chest builders.

2. Sunburst carving looks more complicated than it is, and, though you may never have carved before, you should be able to get a creditable job. Practice beforehand on a scrap of face wood until you have the hang of it. Here are suggested steps:

   a) Make full-size patterns on stiff paper.

   b) Mark with a compass the circular area to be dished out.

   c) Scoop out this area with a shallow sweep gouge — or secure the drawer front to the lathe faceplate and turn it out.

   d) Lay off the rays and inner circle of the diamond points (chip carve the latter).

   e) Cut the rays with a parting tool and round them over with a bent-back inside-bevel gouge.

3. These Queen Anne legs are square in cross section at the knee and gradually work into a circular section about 8 in. from the floor. A lathe and off-center turning may be used to turn the feet and ankles, or the job may be done by hand altogether.

4. The tenons are all pinned. Drill 3/16-in. holes about 3/8 in. from the edge of the leg and about 1¼ in. deep. Cut pins 3/16 by 3/16 by 1½ in., and chamfer two or four sides of one end. Dip the pins in glue to a depth of about 3/8 in., and drive them into the holes as you would drive a nail. Do this while the work is in clamps, and then the clamps may be removed. Carefully cut off the projecting ends of the pins with a saw that has no set to avoid scratching the finished surfaces. A saw good enough for this job and kept for cutting off pins may be bought at a dime store.

5. Drawer members have been billed with a clearance of 1/16 in. side to side and vertically for fronts, while the sides and backs have been given 1/8 in. This conforms to the original and is good practice generally with lip drawers.

6. The top or crown molding is nailed on the original and the nail holes are plugged. The molding may be put on with screws driven in from the back. No glue should be used under the side molding pieces except for about 2 in. at the front, to allow for contraction and expansion of the chest sides.

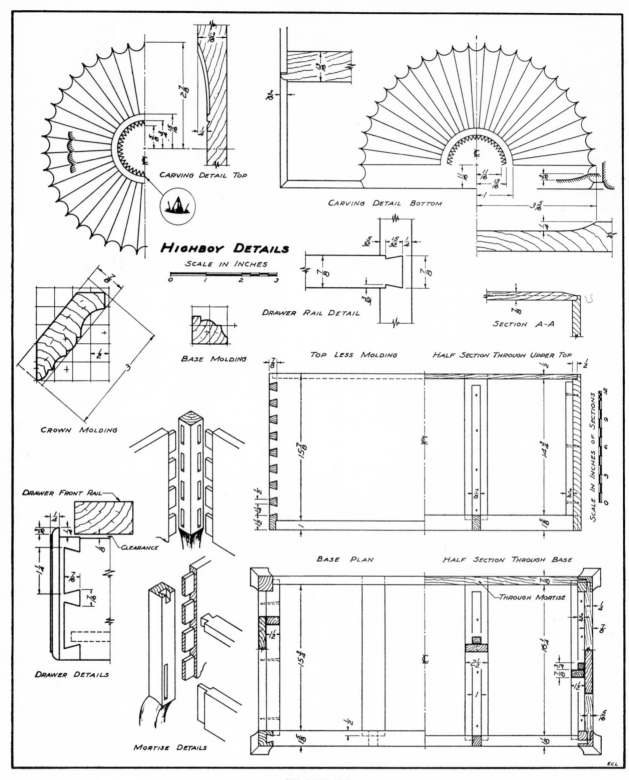

CARVING DETAIL TOP

CARVING DETAIL BOTTOM

HIGHBOY DETAILS

SCALE IN INCHES
0   1   2   3

DRAWER RAIL DETAIL

SECTION A-A

BASE MOLDING

TOP LESS MOLDING

HALF SECTION THROUGH UPPER TOP

CROWN MOLDING

SCALE IN INCHES OF SECTIONS
0   3   6   9   12

DRAWER FRONT RAIL

Clearance

BASE PLAN

HALF SECTION THROUGH BASE

Through Mortise

DRAWER DETAILS

MORTISE DETAILS

ECL

PLATE 27

Bill of Materials

PIECES	ARTICLE	KIND OF WOOD	THICKNESS	WIDTH	LENGTH	REMARKS
	Top					
1	Top	Pine	½	15⅞	34½	Dovetail into sides.
2	Sides	Cherry	⅞	16⅞	39⅛	
1	Top facing	Cherry	1	3⅛	34	Dovetail ends.
1	Molding	Cherry	⅞	3	39	Miter to fit case.
2	Moldings	Cherry	⅞	3	19½	Miter to fit case.
2	Drawer rails	Cherry	⅞	1⅝	11½	Dovetail ends.
2	Drawer stiles	Cherry	⅞	1⅝	8⅝	7⅝ in. between dovetails
5	Drawer rails	Cherry	⅞	1⅝	34	Dovetail ends.
2	Drawer runners	Pine	⅞	2½	16⅜	15⅜ in. between tenons
2	Drawer runners	Pine	⅞	2½	15¾	14¾ in. between tenons
2	Drawer runners	Pine	⅞	1¾	15¾	14¾ in. between tenons
18	Drawer runners and guides	Pine	¾	⅞	14½	
1	Back	Pine	½	12	33¾	
1	Back	Pine	⅞	27	33¾	
1	Front	Cherry	13/16	7 13/16	10 15/16	Carve full sunburst.
2	Sides	Pine	½	7½	16⅛	
1	Back	Pine	½	6¾	10 7/16	
1	Bottom	Pine	½	16	9 15/16	Groove ¼ in. into sides and front.
4	Fronts	Cherry	13/16	3 9/16	10 11/16	
8	Sides	Pine	½	3¼	16⅛	
4	Backs	Pine	½	2½	10 9/16	
4	Bottoms	Pine	½	16	9 11/16	
1	Front	Cherry	13/16	5 1/16	33 3/16	
1	Front	Cherry	13/16	5 11/16	33 3/16	
1	Front	Cherry	13/16	6 7/16	33 3/16	
1	Front	Cherry	13/16	7 1/16	33 3/16	
2	Sides	Pine	½	4¾	16⅛	
2	Sides	Pine	½	5⅜	16⅛	
2	Sides	Pine	½	6⅛	16⅛	
2	Sides	Pine	½	6¾	16⅛	
1	Back	Pine	½	4	32 11/16	
1	Back	Pine	½	4⅝	32 11/16	
1	Back	Pine	½	5⅜	32 11/16	
1	Back	Pine	½	6	32 11/16	
4	Bottoms	Pine	½	16	32 3/16	
	Base					
4	Legs	Cherry	2½	2½	32½	
1	Top drawer rail	Cherry	1	1⅝	35¼	33¾ in. between dovetails
2	Drawer stiles	Cherry	1	1⅛	7¾	6¾ in. between dovetails
1	Apron	Cherry	1⅛	4	36¼	33¾ in. between tenons
2	Sides	Cherry	⅞	11¾	17½	15 in. between tenons
1	Back	Pine	⅞	11¾	36¼	33¾ in. between tenons
2	Drawer top runners	Pine	1	2½	17⅛	⅞-in. tenon, one end; ½-in. tenon, other end
2	Drawer runners	Pine	⅞	2½	17⅝	⅞-in. tenon, one end; ½-in. tenon, other end
2	Drawer top runners	Pine	1	1½	16¾	15¾ in. between tenons
2	Drawer runners	Pine	⅞	1½	17¼	16¼ in. between tenons
2	Drawer guides	Pine	¾	¾	15	
2	Drawer guides	Pine	¾	1	15½	
	Drawers					
1	Front	Cherry	13/16	6 15/16	10 15/16	
2	Fronts	Cherry	13/16	6 15/16	11 1/16	
6	Sides	Pine	½	6⅝	16⅛	
1	Back	Pine	½	5⅞	10 7/16	
2	Backs	Pine	½	5⅞	10 9/16	
1	Bottom	Pine	½	16	9 15/16	
2	Bottoms	Pine	½	16	10 1/16	
1	Base top molding	Cherry	¾	1	36½	Miter and nail to base; set and plug holes with cherry.
2	Base top moldings	Cherry	¾	1	18	

Hardware: 10 drawer pulls, large (Ball, No. 12); 4 large escutcheons to match; 4 small pulls; 2 brass knobs, ⅝-in. diameter (Ball, No. 315); 4 till locks, ⅞-in. selvedge to key pin

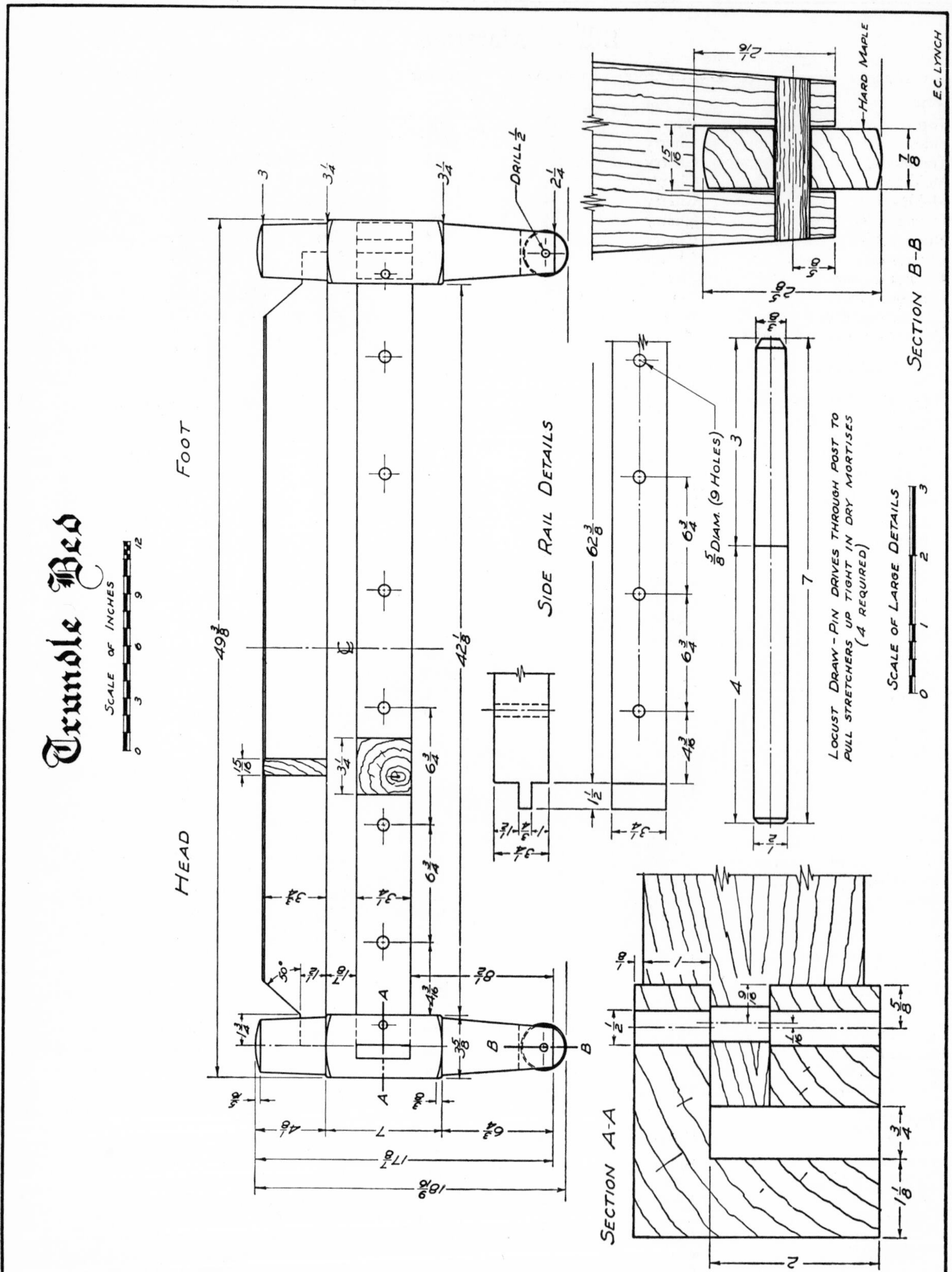
Trundle Bed
Scale of Inches
Head
Foot
Side Rail Details
Drill 1/2
5/8 Diam. (9 Holes)
Locust Draw-Pin drives through post to pull stretchers up tight in dry mortises (4 required)
Scale of Large Details
Section A-A
Section B-B
Hard Maple
E.C. Lynch

PLATE 28

TRUNDLE BED

The word *trundle* is Anglo-Saxon, meaning a small wheel. This old trundle bed has been handed down through many generations of an old Virginia family and yet rolls easily on its hard-maple trundles. It was originally stained mahogany, evidently to match the bed under which it was rolled away, but when the photograph for this book was taken it was natural poplar once more but soon to become walnut in color.

Some trundle beds were made to roll out from under the foot of a large bed instead of from the side.

This bed is an example of the cord bed whose cords were threaded through holes bored in rails and stretches rather than over hardwood pegs. It is assembled with all dry joints, draw pins serving to secure foot- and head-end members, the cords being relied upon to bind ends and rails into a unit.

Bill of Materials

PIECES	ARTICLE	KIND OF WOOD	THICKNESS	WIDTH	LENGTH	REMARKS
4	Posts	Poplar	3⅝	3⅝	17⅞	
2	Head and foot boards	Poplar	$\frac{15}{16}$	3¾	45⅝	42⅛ in. between tenons
2	Stretchers	Poplar	3¼	3¼	45⅝	42⅛ in. between tenons
2	Side rails	Poplar	3¼	3¼	65⅜	62⅜ in. between tenons
4	Trundles	Maple	⅞	2¾	2¾	Turn to 2⅝ diameter, drill center hole ½ in., and sand or ream out to free fit on pins.
4	Trundle pins	Locust	½	½	2½	Turn.
4	Stretcher draw pins	Locust	½	½	7	Turn.

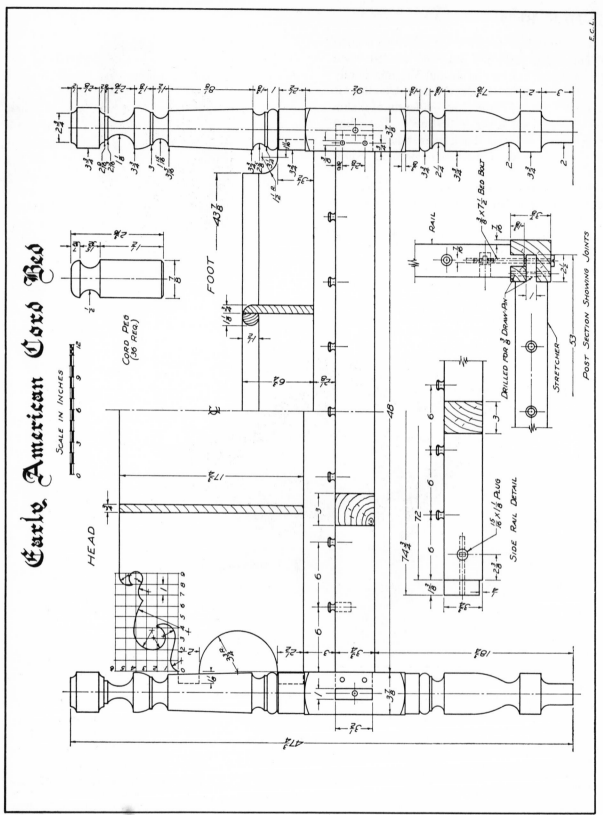

Early American Cord Bed

CORD PEG
(36 REQ.)

SCALE IN INCHES

HEAD

FOOT

RAIL

STRETCHER

POST SECTION SHOWING JOINTS

DRILLED FOR ⅜ DRAW-PIN

¾ X 7½ BED BOLT

SIDE RAIL DETAIL

15/16 X 1⅛ PLUG

PLATE 29

EARLY AMERICAN CORD BED

That our ancestors made beds like this old cord bed out of yellow poplar is no indication of a scarcity of walnut or cherry or maple, but evidence, rather, that the wood was appreciated. Yellow poplar or tulipwood, used to make these cord beds, is almost as soft as white pine but has a more uniform texture. It lends portability to massive things like these bedposts because of its light weight, and is readily stained to pass for the much heavier and more expensive mahogany. The old red stain had been removed from this bed in the process of refinishing.

Cording a bed was not a long or difficult chore. The cords were put on grid fashion and tightened, or the slack was removed by pressing down on one course after the other finally stretching out the accumulated looseness at the head or foot and side. The soft inside shucks of corn were always saved to renew the bedding at least once a year. To this "springs" of corn shucks or straw was added a "mattress" of one or two or more feather or down ticks.

CONSTRUCTION NOTES

1. The craftsman may experience difficulty in obtaining pieces of yellow poplar 4 in. square in some sections of the country. Finished either natural or with a light stain, it will be a striking piece of work.

2. Many craftsmen may not find a lathe large enough to turn the posts. If a commercial-sized lathe is not available for use, the posts can be turned on one of the larger home-workshop lathes provided with a temporary bed extension of sufficient length to gain the required distance between centers. Use a slower speed and lighter cut than usual on a lightweight lathe, after having braced it securely, and the job can be done.

3. The same draw-pin construction is used here as in the trundle bed. No glue but dry joints were used throughout, enabling the bed to be completely disassembled for moving or storing.

Bill of Materials

PIECES	ARTICLE	KIND OF WOOD	THICKNESS	WIDTH	LENGTH	REMARKS
4	Posts	Poplar	3⅞	3⅞	48¾	1 in. for spur center
1	Headboard	Poplar	¾	17¾	50¼	48 in. between tenons
1	Footboard	Poplar	¾	6¾	50¼	48 in. between tenons
1	Footboard roll	Poplar	1⅛	1½	43⅞	
2	Stretchers	Yellow pine	3	3¾	53	48 in. between tenons
2	Side rails	Yellow pine	3	3¾	74¾	72 in. between tenons
36	Pegs	Hickory	⅞	⅞	2³⁄₁₆	Turn.
8	Draw pins	Hickory	⅜	⅜	7	Taper.

Hardware: 4 bed bolts, 6-in.; and oblong nuts

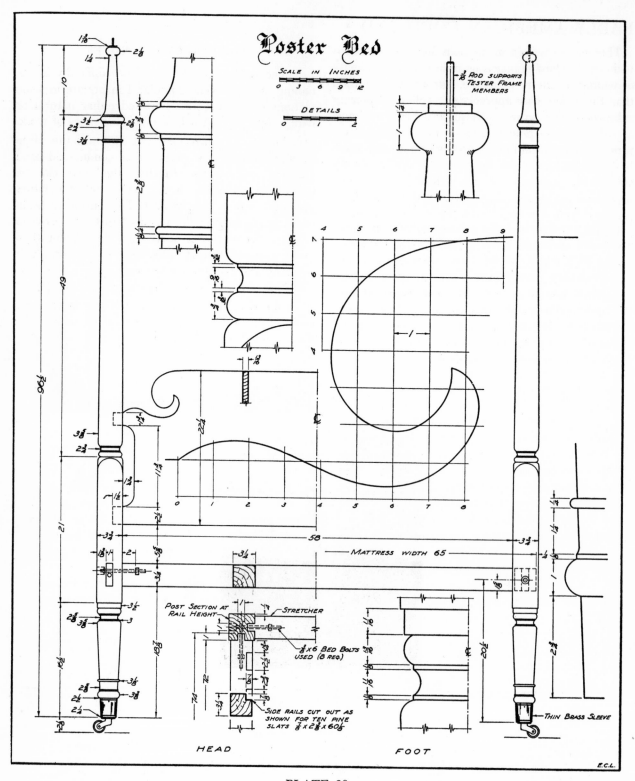

Poster Bed

SCALE IN INCHES

DETAILS

³⁄₈ ROD SUPPORTS TESTER FRAME MEMBERS

MATTRESS WIDTH 65

58

POST SECTION AT RAIL HEIGHT

STRETCHER

³⁄₄ X 6 BED BOLTS USED (8 REQ)

SIDE RAILS CUT OUT AS SHOWN FOR TEN PINE SLATS ⁷⁄₈ X 2⅝ X 60½

THIN BRASS SLEEVE

HEAD

FOOT

E.C.L.

PLATE 30

POSTER BED

This bed is especially valuable because all four posts were turned from the same curly maple log, imparting to all a beautiful figure throughout their length. The bed was discovered near Clemson, South Carolina, and was the property of Professor Hale Houston, beloved professor of Civil Engineering at Clemson and later at Washington and Lee University at Lexington, Virginia.

CONSTRUCTION NOTES

1. Held together by bolts running both ways, this massive bed comes all apart and so is easier to move or store than might be expected. All joints are dry joints, including those of the mahogany headboard.

2. This was never a cord bed but depends on ten yellow-pine slats to uphold whatever bedding was deemed necessary or desirable. Slats notch into upper surface of side rails as shown in detail.

3. A builder of this bed must have ceilings 8½ ft. high, and a heavy lathe with distance enough between centers to turn the posts. The writer saw a lathe specially built for this purpose. Aside from a few bolts, its only metal parts were its headstock and tailstock spindles, the latter a large bolt. Everything else was wood, including the oil-soaked dogwood headstock-spindle bearings. The steady rest was a piece of lumber 2½ by 10 by 24 in., standing on edge. The bed was two pieces of pine 3 by 10 in., held about 4 in. apart; legs resembled those of a very large sawhorse; power from an ancient Fairbanks-Morse engine. A ¾-h.p. electric motor would turn the posts of this bed in such a lathe.

4. Original rails are only 72 in. long between tenons. Modern springs are about 74 in. and some clearance is needed, an inch at each end being enough. The original bed has now especially made box springs cut out around the foot posts, so that a spring length of 75 in. is obtained. These springs rest on the side rails flush with the outside edges to give a width of 65 in. Such an arrangement eliminates the need for slats.

5. Brass bed-bolt covers, although not on the original, will improve and dignify the bed's appearance.

Bill of Materials

PIECES	ARTICLE	KIND OF WOOD	THICKNESS	WIDTH	LENGTH	REMARKS
4	Posts	Maple	3¾	3¾	96½	Turn.
2	Stretchers	Maple	3¼	3¼	60	58 in. between tenons
2	Side rails	Maple	3¼	3¼	74	72 in. between tenons
1	Headboard	Mahogany	13/16	22¼	61	No shoulders on tenons
10	Slats	Yellow pine	⅞	2⅜	60⅛	

Hardware: 8 bed bolts, ⅜ by 6 in., with oblong nuts; 4 heavy brass casters; 4 thin brass ferrules, 2¾ in. long, 2½ in. o.d. at top, 2¼ in. o.d. at bottom; 4 metal pins, 3/16 by 2½; 6 bed-bolt covers, brass (Ball, No. 452)

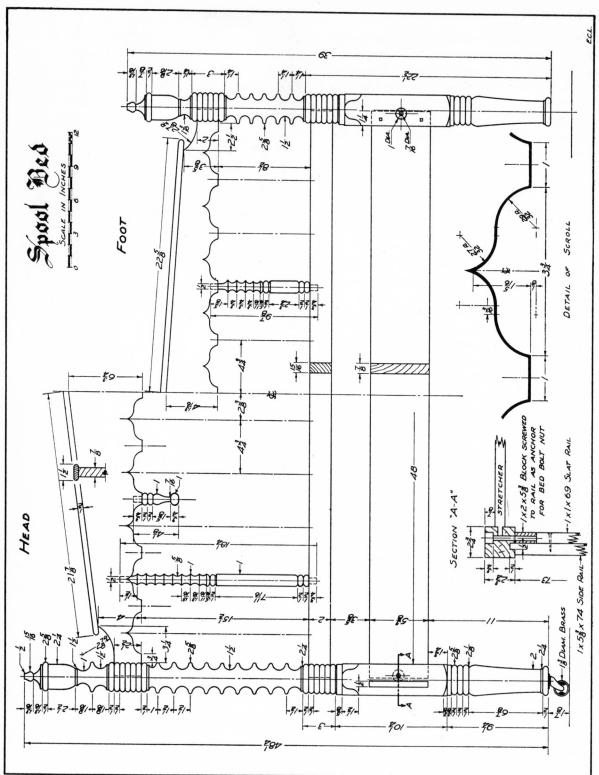

Spool Bed

Scale in Inches

Foot

Head

Detail of Scroll

Section "A-A"

1x2x5⅜ Block screwed to rail as anchor for bed bolt nut

Stretcher

1x1x69 Slat Rail

1x5⅝x74 Side Rail

1⅜ Diam. Brass

PLATE 31

SPOOL BED

This walnut spool bed was copied in an old country home in Augusta County, Virginia. It is just a hundred years old, a modern piece in that old Scotch-Irish community.

The drawing was made dimension for dimension from the original. The measurements may have to be changed to take different springs. With ¼-in. spacer strips added to the inside top edge of the rails, open-coil springs will rest on the rails to give a mattress height of about 30 in. If springs are to rest on rails, the rail width may be reduced and slats eliminated.

CONSTRUCTION NOTES

1. Due to the difficulty of laying out and making mortises on turned pieces, you may prefer to make all mortises before the pieces are turned – while still square – and dry-plug them with softwood. These plugs are easy to bore out after turning.

2. There are no shoulders on the tenons of head and foot boards and center stretchers – entire pieces mortise in to a depth of 1¼ in.

3. The turned portion of the posts and all spools and pendants may not only be sanded but finished and rubbed down in the lathe, if the work is done before the centers are cut off. Tape the tenons of the spools and pendants with masking tape to keep the finishing materials off.

4. Dry assemble the entire piece before gluing and clamping, to make sure the bed will be square after it has been glued up.

Bill of Materials

PIECES	ARTICLE	KIND OF WOOD	THICKNESS	WIDTH	LENGTH	REMARKS
2	Head posts	Walnut	2¾	2¾	48¾	½ in. for lathe center
2	Foot posts	Walnut	2¾	2¾	39½	½ in. for lathe center
1	Headboard	Walnut	⅞	6¾	50½	1¼-in. tenons, each end
2	Headboard caps	Walnut	½	1½	21⅞	Miter at ridge.
10	Headboard spindles	Walnut	1	1	18¾	½ in. for lathe centers
9	Headboard pendants	Walnut	1	1	4⅝	½ in. for lathe centers
1	Footboard	Walnut	⅞	4$^{13}/_{16}$	50½	1¼-in. tenons, each end
2	Footboard caps	Walnut	½	1½	22⅝	Miter at ridge.
9	Footboard spindles	Walnut	1	1	10⅜	½ in. for lathe centers
1	Foot stretcher	Walnut	⅞	5⅜	50½	48 in. between tenons
1	Head stretcher	Poplar	⅞	5⅜	50½	48 in. between tenons
2	Center stretchers	Walnut	$^{15}/_{16}$	2	50½	48 in. between tenons
2	Side rails	Walnut	1	5⅜	74	73 in. between tenons
4	Rail blocks	Poplar	1	2	5⅜	Screwed to rail ends inside as anchors for bed bolts
2	Slat rails	Poplar	1	1	69	Glue and nail to inside lower edge of rail.
7	Slats	Yellow pine	¾	2½	50⅝	

Hardware: 4 brass wheel casters; 4 bed bolts, ⅜ by 5, with nuts; 2 brass bed-bolt covers

Small Chippendale Mirror

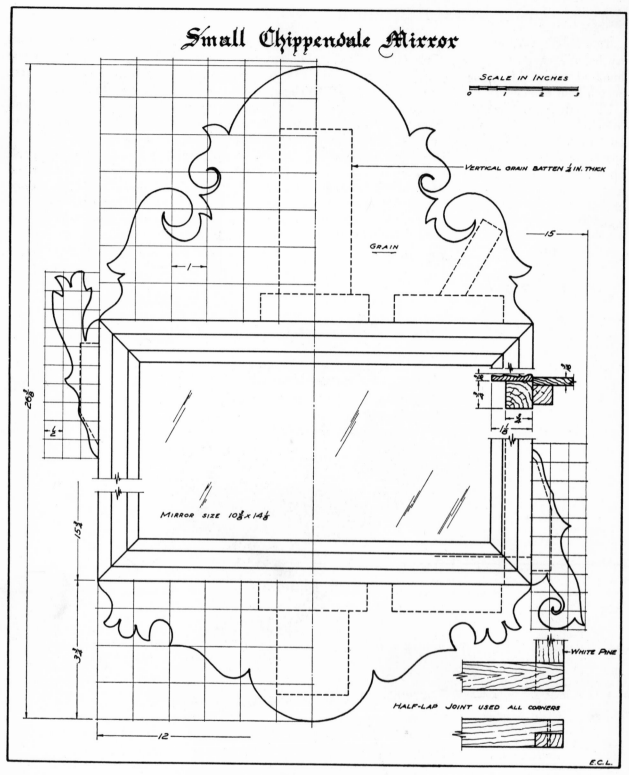

SCALE IN INCHES
0 1 2 3

VERTICAL GRAIN BATTEN ½ IN. THICK

GRAIN

—15—

—1—

26⅜

⅜

15¾

3¾

MIRROR SIZE 10⅜ x 14⅝

½

1⅛

WHITE PINE

HALF-LAP JOINT USED ALL CORNERS

—12—

E.C.L.

PLATE 32

SMALL CHIPPENDALE MIRROR

In the state of Virginia one occasionally finds himself face to face with a person whose ancestry is intimately linked with the very beginnings of this country. The owner of this Chippendale mirror is a seventh-generation direct descendant of William Byrd II. The mirror did not belong to William Byrd but to another illustrious ancestor of its owner in whose family it has been for some one hundred and fifty years.

The several ornaments were traced from the original piece to obtain the drawing shown. Thus the symmetry of the curves executed by the craftsman of that time, long gone, is preserved for interest in our day.

CONSTRUCTION NOTES

1. The use of white pine for the supporting wood has the distinct advantages of assuring a lighter-weight article than could have been made by using solid mahogany, as well as a cheaper one.

2. The use of a half-lap joint, pinned, gave such strength to the original that it is perfectly intact today. The stability of white pine is reflected in the still tight and perfect mitered joints of the mahogany overlay.

3. The shallow surface decoration on the frame

members suggests the work of a scratch stock, though a molding plane may have been used.

4. Mirror glass ⅛ in. thick is recommended as being in keeping with the thin glass used in the original.

Bill of Materials

PIECES	ARTICLE	KIND OF WOOD	THICKNESS	WIDTH	LENGTH	REMARKS
2	Frame tops and bottoms	White pine	¾	¾	12	Use half-lap joint.
2	Frame sides	White pine	¾	¾	15¾	Use half-lap joint.
2	Frame facing strips	Mahogany	3⁄16	1⅛	12	Miter and glue to pine frame.
2	Frame facing strips	Mahogany	3⁄16	1⅛	15¾	Miter and glue to pine frame.
1	Top ornament	Mahogany	3⁄16	6⅞	12	Cut to pattern.
1	Bottom ornament	Mahogany	3⁄16	3¾	12	Cut to pattern.
2	Top side ornaments	Mahogany	3⁄16	1 5⁄16	5	Cut to pattern.
2	Bottom side ornaments	Mahogany	3⁄16	1½	5	Cut to pattern.
1	Glue block	White pine	9⁄16	9⁄16	12	Makes four.
1	Glue block	White pine	9⁄16	¾	18	Makes six.
1	Batten	White pine	¼	2	7	One 4½ in. long; one 2½ in. long
1	Batten	White pine	¼	⅝	4½	Makes two.
1	Back	Yellow pine	⅛	10½	14¼	

Hardware: mirror size, 10⅜ by 14⅛

87

Grandfather Clock

SCALE IN INCHES

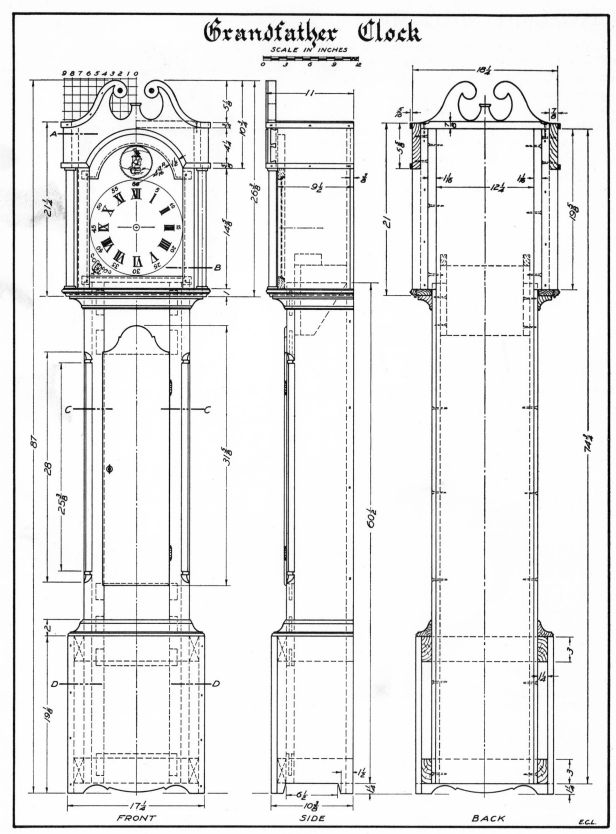

FRONT

SIDE

BACK

E.C.L.

PLATE 33

GRANDFATHER CLOCK

Although copied in the South where it has been for many years, this graceful old clock came from New England. It is made of white pine throughout, now a rich brown amber color from age. The basswood face is painted pale blue. Beautifully designed hands are cast pewter. The works are of wood, made

Bill of Materials

PIECES	ARTICLE	KIND OF WOOD	THICKNESS	WIDTH	LENGTH	REMARKS
	Hood					
1	Scroll cap front	White pine	1	10 3/4	18 1/4	
2	Cap sides	White pine	7/8	5 5/8	10 7/16	Dovetails cut one end.
2	Hood sides	White pine	7/8	9 1/8	21	3/8 by 2 1/4-in. tenons one end. Rabbet one edge 1/8 by 7/8 in. for door. Pair up.
1	Hood frame front	White pine	3/4	1 15/16	17 1/4	
2	Hood frame sides	White pine	3/4	1 15/16	9 5/8	Tenon one end 3/8 by 1 1/4 by 1 1/4
1	Hood frame molding	White pine	13/16	1	19 1/4	Miter around hood frame.
2	Hood frame moldings	White pine	13/16	1	11 5/16	Miter around hood frame.
2	Columns	White pine	1	1	15 5/8	Turn. 14 1/8 in. between 3/8-in. diameter tenons
4	Column caps and bases	White pine	1/4	1 1/4	1/4	3/8-in. hole through center
2	Scroll moldings	White pine	5/16	2 3/4	10	Cut to pattern. Miter around hood cap.
2	Scroll moldings	White pine	5/16	3/4	11	Cut to pattern. Miter around hood cap.
1	Scroll cap	White pine	1/4	1 5/16	1 5/16	
1	Hood-door arch molding	White pine	5/16	4 7/8	13	Cut to radius above door arch.
2	Hood-door arch moldings	White pine	5/16	5/8	3 3/4	Miter to above.
2	Cap side moldings	White pine	5/16	5/8	11	Miter one end.
1	Arch filler strip	White pine	1/4	4 7/8	16 1/4	
1	Hood top	White pine	7/8	9 3/4	16 1/8	
2	Wings	White pine	3/8	1 7/8	19 5/8	
2	Door stiles	White pine	7/8	1 1/2	14 5/8	
1	Door rail	White pine	7/8	5 1/2	13 5/8	Cut to pattern, 11 5/8 in. between tenons.
1	Door rail	White pine	7/8	1 1/2	13 5/8	11 5/8 in. between tenons
	Case					
2	Sides	White pine	1	7 3/8	60 1/2	
2	Frame stiles	White pine	1	2 1/2	60 1/2	
1	Frame top rail	White pine	1	8 3/4	10 1/4	8 1/4 in. between tenons
1	Frame center rail	White pine	1	10	10 1/4	8 1/4 in. between tenons
1	Frame bottom rail	White pine	1	3 1/2	10 1/4	8 1/4 in. between tenons
2	Quarter columns	White pine	7/8	7/8	25 3/8	
1	Door	White pine	7/8	8 1/2	31 5/8	
1	Top molding	White pine	1 3/4	1 3/4	16 3/4	Miter around case.
2	Top moldings	White pine	1 3/4	1 3/4	10 1/8	Miter around case.
1	Plinth molding	White pine	2	2	17 1/4	Miter around case.
2	Plinth moldings	White pine	2	2	10 1/4	Miter around case.
1	Plinth front	White pine	3/4	17 1/4	19 1/8	
2	Plinth sides	White pine	3/4	9 1/2	19 1/8	
2	Spacers	White pine	1 1/4	3	13 1/4	
4	Spacers	White pine	1 1/4	3	9 1/2	
1	Back	White pine	7/8	12 1/4	74 3/4	
2	Back top strips	White pine	7/8	1 1/16	19 5/8	
2	Bracket sides	White pine	3/4	5 3/4	8 1/2	These pieces, outlined in side and back views, will vary with works used and so are not detailed.
1	Bracket front	White pine	3/4	8 1/2	11 1/4	
2	Bracket caps	White pine	3/4	1 3/8	3 1/2	

Hardware: 2 brass rosettes (Ball, No. 460); 2 hinges, broad butt brass, 1 1/2 in.; 1 cupboard turn (Ball, No. 350, 1 1/4 in.); 1 cupboard lock, small, for hood door; 1 window glass, 12 by 18, cut to shape; 2 brass pivots, homemade

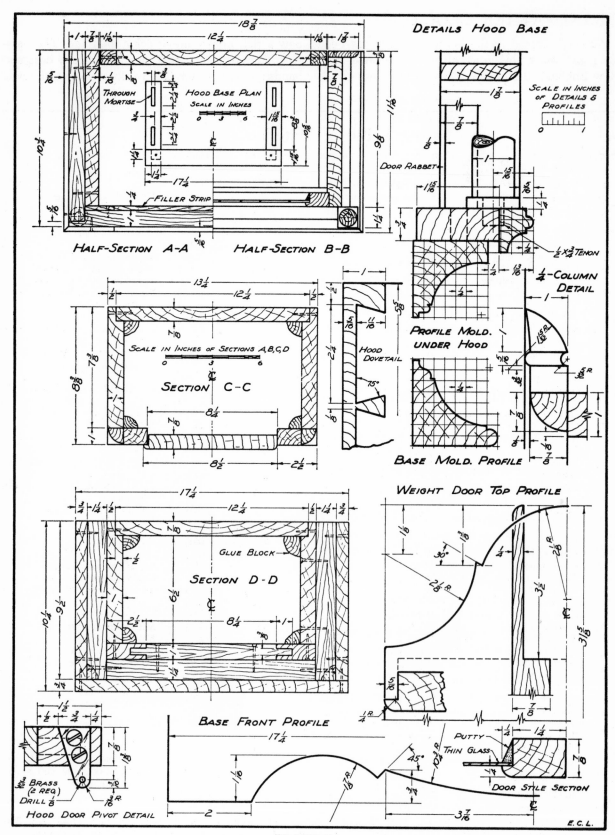

DETAILS HOOD BASE

HOOD BASE PLAN
SCALE IN INCHES

THROUGH MORTISE

FILLER STRIP

HALF-SECTION A-A   HALF-SECTION B-B

SCALE IN INCHES OF DETAILS & PROFILES

DOOR RABBET

½ × ¾ TENON

¼-COLUMN DETAIL

SECTION C-C

SCALE IN INCHES OF SECTIONS A,B,C,D

HOOD DOVETAIL

PROFILE MOLD. UNDER HOOD

BASE MOLD. PROFILE

SECTION D-D

GLUE BLOCK

WEIGHT DOOR TOP PROFILE

BRASS (2 REQ)
DRILL

HOOD DOOR PIVOT DETAIL

BASE FRONT PROFILE

PUTTY
THIN GLASS

DOOR STILE SECTION

E.C.L.

PLATE 34

90

to run thirty hours. Two weights are pulled up by cords held taut by ancient lead sinkers, and so no key is used. The slow, measured tick of this old clock is a comforting sound and friendly, too, if you are alone. A sweet-toned bell rings the hours.

Well proportioned and graceful, it is a simple case to build. The parts were assembled with glue and nails and glue blocks, and no attempt was made to hide old square nailheads.

Eight-day brass works are available for tall clocks, complete with striking mechanism, so that there is a choice between works that tick and strike and the silence of electric works. Drawings of the face and hands have been included to further the cause of accuracy in reproduction.

In the drawings and bill the writer shows the door of the hood made to open. The original clock door will not open, nor does it have hinges or pivots. Access to the face was occasioned only when the hands wanted setting, and so the entire hood was removed. However, the complete and separate door is there and could be made to open on the original.

CONSTRUCTION NOTES

1. The hood or bonnet of the clock rests on the top case molding where it is free to be slid off. Two $\frac{7}{8}$ by $1\frac{1}{16}$-in. strips, nailed to each side of the case back, project to hold down the hood frame at the back.

2. Not all home shops are equipped with a shaper that will make moldings as large as that used on this clock, nor do we have the old hand planes used by our ancestors. Such lacks need not deter anyone who wants to build this piece. Most of the work on all three of these shaped moldings can be done on a circular saw.[1] They may be made also with hand tools alone, such as rabbet plane, block plane, wide shallow gouges, and a couple of narrow deep gouges.

3. Build the case frame first and then glue it to the sides. The stiles are cut away to receive the quarter columns. These are not decorated in any way and are no more than $\frac{7}{8}$-in. quarter round molding. Carve the decorative caps and bases of the columns into the stiles.

---

[1] *Machine Woodworking*, by Herman Hjorth, p. 72.

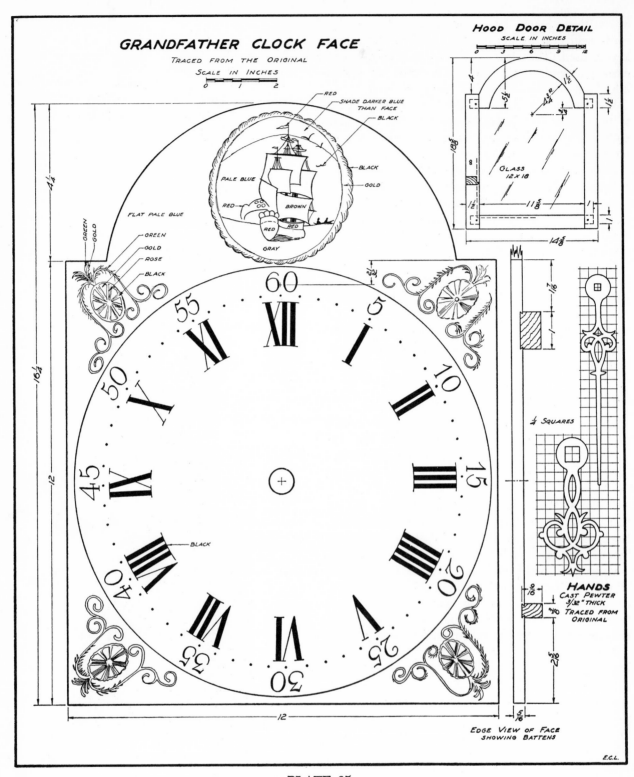

GRANDFATHER CLOCK FACE

TRACED FROM THE ORIGINAL

SCALE IN INCHES

HOOD DOOR DETAIL

SCALE IN INCHES

GLASS 12 x 18

HANDS
CAST PEWTER
3/32" THICK
TRACED FROM
ORIGINAL

¼ SQUARES

EDGE VIEW OF FACE
SHOWING BATTENS

E.C.L.

PLATE 35

BIBLIOGRAPHY

Southern Antiques by Paul H. Burroughs, 1931, Garrett & Massie, Inc., Richmond, Va.

Southern Furniture 1640–1820 by The Magazine Antiques, 1952

How to Design Period Furniture by Franklin H. Gottshall, 1937, Bruce

Design for the Craftsman by Franklin H. Gottshall, 1940, Bruce

Reproduction of Antique Furniture by Herman Hjorth, Bruce

Principles of Woodworking by Herman Hjorth, Bruce

Colonial Furniture by Wenger and Shea, Bruce

American Windsors by Wallace Nutting, Macmillan

Treasury of American Furniture (3 vols.) by Wallace Nutting, Macmillan

Machine Woodworking by Herman Hjorth, Bruce

INDEX